Believers' Prayers and Promises

D1361947

Believers' Prayers and Promises

by
CLIFT RICHARDS
with
LLOYD HILDEBRAND

Victory House, Inc.
Tulsa, Oklahoma

This book was previously published in trade-size format under the title *God's Special Promises to Me.*

BELIEVERS' PRAYERS AND PROMISES
Copyright © 2000 by K. & C. International, Inc.
ISBN 0-932081-71-1

Published by Victory House, Inc.
P.O. Box 700238
Tulsa, Oklahoma 74170
(918) 747-5009

Contents

THE POWER OF
BIBLE MEDITATION

> *Blessed is the man who walks not in the counsel of the ungodly, nor stands in the path of sinners, nor sits in the seat of the scornful; But his delight is in the law of the Lord, and in his law he meditates day and night. He shall be like a tree planted by the rivers of water, that brings forth its fruit in season, Whose leaf also shall not wither; And whatever he does shall prosper. (Ps. 1:1-3, NKJV)*

What Bible Mediation Is

The process of meditation has often been compared to a cow chewing its cud. A cow, as you know, is a ruminant in that it has a four-chambered stomach that permits it to swallow food, partially digest it, bring it up again, swallow once more, and so forth, until the process of digestion is complete. This is an effective analogy to use in explaining Bible meditation.

As we meditate on a promise from God, we taste its flavorful truth, chew on it awhile, swallow it, bring it up again, chew some more, swallow, and so forth. This is the process of spiritual digestion that takes place when we meditate upon the promises of God. Rumination, contemplation, and meditation are related terms. Ruminating (meditating) on God's promises involves going over their truth again and again in our minds, hearts, and spirits. It is a slow and deliberate process that involves musing (chewing) on the truth over and over again.

This is what God was referring to when He told Joshua:

> *This Book of the Law shall not depart from your mouth, but you shall meditate in it day and night, that you may observe to do according to all that is written in it. For then you will make your way prosperous, and then you will have good success (Josh. 1:8, NKJV).*

There is evidence to suggest that the Hebrew root from which the word meditate stems includes saying, or speaking something over and over to one's self. Therefore, one facet of our meditation of God's Word is to feed upon that Word by saying the Scripture promise over and over to ourselves. As we do this, the seed of the Word will sink way down into the good ground of our heart and take root there. As that seed of the Word begins to grow we continue to water it through further meditation, prayer, praise, and thanksgiving. Then, in the process of time, it will be able to bring forth God's intended harvest.

Take each of the following promises one at a time. Read them, chew on them, reflect on them, memorize them. Continually meditate upon their truths. Bring them up over and over again. Contemplate the rich love that gives them to you. In so doing you will eventually digest their truth — a process that will energize your faith, give you strength and health, and enable you to stand firm on God's Word. Think on these promises often as you go about the daily course of your life. Personalize God's promises by remembering that they are for you.

Reaping God's Promises

God is a promise-keeper, and you can be a promise-reaper. The Bible is a sacred promise book from your heavenly Father. He is the Giver of every good and perfect gift. "Do not be deceived, my beloved brethren. Every good gift and every perfect gift is from above, and comes down from the Father of lights, with whom there is no variation or shadow of turning" (James 1:16-17, NKJV).

God never changes. "For I am the Lord, I change not" (Mal. 3:6). "Jesus Christ is the same yesterday, today, and forever" (Heb. 13:8, NKJV). You can count on God. His Word is His bond. "For I am ready to perform My word" (Jer. 1:12, NKJV). His love for you is constant. He is Jehovah-Shammah, the God who is always there.

The Word of God is a personal letter from your Father in heaven. It is addressed to you. The Bible speaks of God's eternal covenant with you and with every member of His family. On almost every page of the Scriptures God has engraved solid promises for you to reap, claim, and appropriate for yourself and your family. These precious promises are for *you* and *yours*!

By meditating on the promises of God, as they are revealed in His Word, your faith is built up (see Rom. 10:17), enabling you to receive each promise in your life. This book is designed to help you to focus on the promises of God instead of the problems of life.

Promise-Centered Living

We used to sing a profoundly simple chorus in Sunday school. It proclaimed, "Every promise in the Book is mine." Sometimes children, unlike many adults, find it easy to accept such a truth because they are trusting by nature. Jesus wants us to have child-like faith when it comes to accepting the promises He has given to us. Every promise in His Book is for *you*!

In our fast-paced society we all too frequently get caught up with stressful demands on our time and other resources. In the process we lose sight of God's promises, focusing instead on issues related to materialism, finances, and other things of this world. This is not God's will for you. He wants you to learn to live His promises.

The epigram at the beginning of this section (Ps. 1:1-3) reveals what happens to us when our lives become promise-centered instead of problem-centered. In these three verses alone we find at least five personal promises to claim and live by. These are promises to you from your heavenly Father:

1. *God will bless you.* God wants to bless your life. He is a God of blessing. It is His nature to bless the ones He loves; in fact, He cannot do otherwise. The promises of His Word are blessings for you to claim.

2. *Meditating on the Word of God will give you the strength and vitality of a tree planted by the river.* The Law of the Lord is the Bible. God wants us to meditate upon His law day and night. We need to read, study, think upon, and memorize the Scriptures. As we do so, we grow strong and tall in the face of the winds of life. The image

employed by the Psalmist implies strength, solidity, permanence, life, health, peace, and longevity. These are the Father's promises to you.

3. *You will be fruitful.* Jesus said, "I chose you and appointed you that you should go and bear fruit, and that your fruit should remain, that whatever you ask the Father in My name He may give you" (John 15:16, NKJV). Bible meditation makes you into a fruitful tree (a fruit-bearing Christian), and when this metamorphosis takes place in your life you will experience the continuing joys of answered prayer. (Getting your prayers answered is actually claiming and receiving the promises of God!) Your life will bear much fruit, and that fruit will last. The fruit of the Spirit, as revealed in Galatians 5, will sustain you and others as you practice promise-centered living. Your love, joy, peace, gentleness, faithfulness, goodness, meekness, self-control (all promises of God for you) will lead others to want what you have.

4. *Your leaf will not wither.* Vitality and strength are part of the inheritance your Father has bequeathed to you. He will renew your strength (see Isa. 40:31), and He will quicken (give life to) your mortal body. (See Rom. 8:11.)

Health, vitality, and longevity are promises from God to you.

5. *Whatever you do will prosper.* Prosperity for the righteous is a major Bible theme in both the Old and New Testaments. The dictionary defines prosperity as "the condition of being successful or thriving." You will be successfully thriving as you walk in the promises of God's Word. God, your heavenly Father, wants to prosper you!

God's Word Cannot Fail

The key to living a blessed life and securing the promises of God is found in Bible meditation. Like prayer, Bible study, praise, and worship, meditating on the promises of the Bible is a vitally important practice for every believer to engage in continually. This is because God's Word cannot fail. For example, the five promises outlined above from Psalms 1, can be rightfully claimed by every person who delights in meditation upon the Word of God.

Jesus assures us, "Heaven and earth will pass away, but My words will by no means pass away" (Matt. 24:35, NKJV). The Word of God is eternal.

The Psalmist stresses the importance of the Word of God when he proclaims, "For You have magnified Your word above all Your name" (Ps. 138:2, NKJV). God's Word is eternal and it is to be highly exalted.

The prophet Isaiah magnifies God's Word by pointing to its purpose and its power. He writes, "For as the rain comes down . . . . So shall My word be that goes forth from My mouth; it shall not return to Me void, But it shall accomplish what I please, And it shall prosper in the thing for which I sent it" (Isa. 55:10-11, NKJV).

God's Word accomplishes God's eternal purposes in your life. It cannot fail; it will never return to Him void.

God stands ready to make His Word good in our lives. He guarantees His Word and He says in Jeremiah1:12 that, ". . . I will hasten my word to perform it."

Seated With Christ

This kind of meditation is empowering. It enables a follower of Jesus Christ to rise above the circumstances of life and gain a heavenly viewpoint. This is true transcendence (rising above or going beyond normal and natural limits). Bible meditation gives us a higher perspective with regard to the problems of life.

One special promise to you from God in heaven relates to this kind of transcendence:

> *And* [God has] *raised us up together, and made us sit together in the heavenly places in Christ Jesus, that in the ages to come He might show the exceeding riches of His grace in His kindness toward us in Christ Jesus.* (Eph. 2:6-7, NIV)

Here again we have special promises from God to you, and you can actualize these promises in your life through Bible meditation:

1. God has raised you up with Christ.

2. He has seated you with Christ in the heavenly realms. (Talk about transcendence!)

3. He will show you the incomparable riches of His grace.

How Firm a Foundation

We are such fortunate people! God loves us, and He wants to bless us. He is our true Father. We have been adopted into His family, and He enables us to share the blessings of sonship with His only begotten Son, our Lord and Savior, Jesus Christ. He promises to give us innumerable spiritual and temporal blessings, and He never fails to keep His promises.

Believers' Prayers and Promises has been written in order to help you gain a deeper relationship with the God of these unlimited promises so that you will be able to experience the showers of His blessing every day of your life. These blessings will come as you meditate upon the promises of God as they are revealed in the Bible. As you read, meditate, and pray you will discover the wealth of promises He has stored up for you. You will learn how to claim His promises, and to incorporate them into your daily living. Your faith will grow and you will take your stand upon His promises, fully trusting that they will never fail. The promises of God will form a firm foundation for your life.

As you read the Bible promises, meditations, and prayers associated with each scriptural topic in this book, you will want to reach out and take hold of God's promises through faith. They are His special, personal promises to you — His child. The promises are there because He loves you. They are for you!

God promises much more to you than you realize. "Eye has not seen, nor ear heard, nor have entered into the heart of man the things which God has prepared for those who love Him — But God has revealed them to us through His Spirit" (1 Cor. 2:9-10, NKJV).

God's promises are life and they are victory. They are spiritual stepping-stones to abundant living in the here-and-now. You do not have to wait until you get to heaven in order to receive them. They are available for you now. Never forget that your Father loves you with an everlasting love. He has so much in store for you, and He always wants the very best for you.

Your joy and excitement will intensify as you realize the full extent of God's personal covenant with you. Your trust in Him will be perfected as you mine the pure gold that is found on the pages of this book. This treasure chest full of sparkling promises will enrich your life in deeply meaningful ways. A higher dimension of living awaits you, and you will never be the same.

You will be amazed to discover what happens when you delight yourself in God's Word. The Psalmist gives us this enduring promise on which to build your life: "The Lord knows the way of the righteous" (Ps. 1:6, NKJV). This entails so much, and every promise in the Bible is connected to this truth. God is watching over you, and all His special promises are yours!

CHILDREN OF THE PROMISE-KEEPER

Through the Lord's mercies we are not consumed, because His compassions fail not. They are new every morning; great is your faithfulness. (Lam. 3:22-23, NKJV)

Great Is His Faithfulness

God is absolutely faithful to every word He speaks. We see His great faithfulness on every page of the Scriptures. He promised to give Abraham a son, and to make of him a mighty nation so that all the nations of the earth would be blessed. (See Gen. 18:19; 21:1; 22:15-18; 26:1-5; Deut. 1:11; and 1 Chron. 16:16.) He led the people of Israel into the Land of Promise. (See Gen. 50:22-25; Exod. 3:17; 12:25; and 32:13.) It was God's covenant with His children that saw them through many trials and tribulations from one generation to the next.

He remembers his covenant forever, the word he commanded, for a thousand generations, the covenant he made with Abraham, the oath he swore to Isaac. He confirmed it to Jacob as a decree, to Israel as an everlasting covenant. (Ps. 105:8-10, NIV)

Throughout the Old Testament God's covenant with His children is viewed as a promise that cannot be broken. His Word is truly inviolable, and He honors all His promises to us. In fact, God's Word (covenant, bond, pledge, promise, commitment, contract) to Israel became the very source, strength, destiny, and purpose of His people. It gave them hope and confidence, and many built their lives upon His Word. Indeed, many staked their lives upon His promises.

God *speaks.* God *says.* God *covenants.* God *promises.* God *performs* These italicized verbs are active. They show how God takes action in your behalf. These active verbs possess incredible power when God is their subject — the One who is taking the action. Each one of these divine actions and interventions take place time and again in the Bible, and the object of each verb is us — the people of God. The one upon whom the action is taken is you. God acts through His Word, and you receive the benefits of that action every time.

Utter Confidence in God

Without question, the inspired writers of the Old Testament were certain that God would be faithful to every word He spoke. This is the believer's stance, and it should be our position in the world today. Isaiah, the ancient prophet, tells us why:

> *The grass withers and the flowers fall, but the word of our God stands forever. (Isa. 40:8, NIV)*

Complete and utter confidence in God and in His Word guided the leaders and prophets of Israel. God gave specific promises to each of the leaders of His people, and He is still doing so today. He called Moses to deliver His people from Egypt. He gave assurances to King David and King Solomon that He would fulfill the vow He gave to Abraham through them. He spoke directly to each of the prophets, reminding them that He would always remain true to His Word. Though each of these divine promises was addressed to specific individuals in particular circumstances, they contain eternal truths and divine principles for each of us to claim because they are rooted in God's initial covenant to Abraham. Therefore, the promises of the Bible apply to each of us who believe in the Lord, and we can appropriate them for our lives on earth and the after-life as well. God wants us to build our lives upon the foundation of His Word. (See Matt. 7:24-27.)

This, then, is the theme of *Believers' Prayers and Promises.* God has given special promises to you. They are for you if you will but believe them, obey them, appropriate them, and stand upon them, no matter what may come your way. God expects you to walk in faith, trusting wholly in His Word and all His promises. The more you focus on His promises the greater your faith will grow, and this process will enable you to take His promises as your own. He will always do His part; He cannot do otherwise. Your responsibility (your response to His ability) is to obey His Word and to trust Him. This, as the hymn declares, is the only way.

> *Trust and obey, For there's no other way, To be happy in Jesus, But to trust and obey.*

Absolute Surrender

Andrew Murray writes, "We have heard it before, but we need to hear it very definitely — the condition of God's blessing is absolute surrender of all into His hands. If our hearts are willing for that, there is no end to what God will do for us, and to the blessing God will bestow."

Absolute surrender means that our lives must be totally consecrated to God and the Lordship of Jesus Christ. Someone has said, "If you want God's best, then you must give Him your best." After all God cared enough to give the very best, His Son, Jesus Christ.

If the cry of our hearts is to be like Jesus and to walk in God's perfect will for our lives, then we will have to walk as Jesus walked. A wonderful example of Jesus' absolute surrender and total consecration to God is illustrated in His prayer to the Father in the Garden of Gesthemene. It was there in the Garden, knowing He faced torture, pain, humiliation, and death, that He prayed, "O My Father, if it is possible, let this cup pass from Me; nevertheless, not as I will, but as You will" (Matt. 26:39, NKJV).

Absolute surrender begins with our individual choice to surrender our life, our will, our self-interest, our everything, to God's plan, purpose, and will for us. We effectively give up control of our lives to God. We choose to be totally dependent upon God. We choose to walk in the ways that are pleasing to God. We choose to allow God to help us to live godly, holy, and sanctified lives.

Jesus said, "I am the vine, you are the branches, He who abides in Me, and I in him, bears much fruit; for without Me you can do nothing" (John 15:5, NKJV). He stresses our utter dependency on Him, and then He gives us a key to answered prayer, "If you abide in Me, and My words abide in you, you will ask what you desire, and it shall be done for you" (John 15:7, NKJV).

Absolute surrender to Jesus Christ involves abiding in Him and letting His words abide in us. When this happens in our lives we are fully able to realize the life-giving truth expressed by the Apostle Paul: "For you were bought with a price; therefore glorify God in your body and in your spirit, which are God's" (1 Cor. 6:20, NKJV). It is absolute surrender to God that qualifies us to truly experience being "children of promise."

Children of the Promise

Many human beings break their promises from time to time. Sometimes individuals will even forget that they made certain promises, such as a promise to pray for a friend, a promise to spend time with a child, a promise to pay a debt, etc. God, however, will never break His pledge to His people. His "promissory note" will always be paid. It is impossible for Him to fail. The saying, "Promises are made to be broken," is totally beyond the purview of God's heart and mind.

You are a child of the promise. The New Testament, like the Old, reveals that God's pledge to His people is forever and ever. A true believer in New Testament times trusted unreservedly in the power of God to fulfill His promises. The Christian knows that God is his/her Father, and that He wants only the best for His children. His purposes for your life are good in every respect. He tells us, "For I know the thoughts that I think toward you, says the Lord, thoughts of peace and not of evil, to give you a future and a hope" (Jer. 29:11, NKJV).

The Apostle Paul gives us a special name, as the people of God. He calls us "children of the promise" (Rom. 9:8-9). It is apparent that the promise he refers to is the covenant God gave to Abraham — a blessing for all Abraham's descendants and heirs, both Jews and Gentiles. Gentile believers are in line for this blessing of the Covenant because our Lord and Savior, Jesus Christ, is the seed of Abraham.

> *The promises were spoken to Abraham and to his seed. The Scripture does not say "and to seeds," meaning many people, but "and to your seed," meaning one person, who is Christ. (Gal. 3:16, NIV)*

In Christ, all of us became sons of God because we believed on His name. (See John 1:12.) Therefore, we are the children to whom the Father's promise is given. As children, then, we are heirs — heirs of God and joint-heirs with Jesus Christ, His only begotten Son. (See Rom. 8:15-17 and John 3:16.) We have been adopted into the family of God, and we are now involved in the fulfillment of His promise on earth. We are the children of the promise!

> *But when the time had fully come, God sent his Son, born of a woman, born under law, to redeem those under law, that we might receive the full rights of sons. Because you are sons, God sent the Spirit of his Son into our hearts, the Spirit who calls out, "Abba, Father."* *(Gal. 4:4-6, NIV)*

Abba is an Aramaic term for "father." It connotes a degree of familiarity between father and child that is often expressed in English by the term "daddy." When a child calls his/her father "daddy," a degree of closeness and familiarity and love cements the bridge between father and child. Whereas the word "father" implies formality and distance, "daddy" implies closeness, warmth, love, and familiarity. Abba is the word from which "abbot" and "abbey" are derived, and we often associate security, protection, deep spirituality, peace, and love with these terms.

God adopted you into His family. He invites you to climb into the safe place of His protection and love. You may express your love to Him as you would to an earthly daddy you love, respect, and enjoy being with. The Spirit of Christ who dwells within you cries out to your heavenly Father, "Abba, Father," terms of endearment, respect, love, and devotion.

In Jesus Christ, all the promises of God are revealed as being true. "For all the promises of God in Him are Yes, and in Him Amen, to the glory of God through us" (2 Cor. 1:20, NKJV). I believe this statement with all my heart, and this is why I have entitled this book, *Believers' Prayers and Promises*. The promises of God are yes and amen to you! All God's promises are for you!

The Spirit of Promise

"My daddy's better than your daddy!" a small child might boast in front of a friend. The child of God can make such a statement very emphatically to those in the world. "Ye are of God, little children, and have overcome them: because greater is he that is in you, than he that is in the world" (1 John 4:4). The One who is within you is the Spirit of promise — the Spirit of God.

The Holy Spirit who indwells you is "the Spirit of promise" (Eph. 1:13). He fulfills God's promises within you. Paul says, ". . . you were sealed with the Holy Spirit of promise, who is the guarantee of our inheritance until the redemption of the purchased possession, to the praise of His glory" (Eph. 1:13-14, NKJV).

Luke concurs with this understanding in both his gospel and the Book of Acts. He wrote, "For the promise [of the Holy Spirit] is to you and to your children, and to all who are afar off, as many as the Lord our God will call" (Acts 2:39, NKJV). The Book of Acts makes it quite clear that the Promise is linked with the covenant God established with Abraham as recorded in Genesis. Stephen, the first Christian martyr, for example, referred to the promise of God as follows: "But when the time of the promise drew near which God had sworn to Abraham, the people grew and multiplied in Egypt ..." (Acts 7:17, NKJV). He then proceeds to recount the history of the Jewish nation, and how God moved among His people, fulfilling His promises to them.

God has called you out of the world, into His kingdom, to walk as children of light. (See Eph. 5:8.) You no longer dwell in the kingdom of darkness. God, your Father, loves you with an everlasting love. As you reflect upon His promises as they are revealed in the Bible and emphasized in this book, your faith will be strengthened, and you will be able to proclaim with Paul, "Faithful is he that calleth you, who also will do it" (1 Thess. 5:24). This statement of faith will emanate from your personal experience with God. You have been sealed with the Spirit of promise; you are a child of the Promise. The promises of God are for you and for your family.

Here is my special, heartfelt prayer for you:

> *Dear Father, bless this reader with a more complete knowledge of your love. Fill him/her with the knowledge of your will in all wisdom and spiritual understanding; that he/she will walk worthy of you, fully pleasing you in all areas of his/her life, being fruitful in every good work, and increasing in the knowledge of you. Strengthen him/her with all might, according to your glorious power, for all patience and longsuffering with joy. Thank you, Father, for your loving promises to this reader. Help him/her to receive the rightful inheritance you have bequeathed to him/her. In Jesus' name, Amen. (Paraphrased from Col. 1:9-11)*

God Answers Prayer

God always answers believing prayer that is based upon His promises. (See the "Other Books of Interest" list in the front of this book in order to find books that will give you a clearer understanding of victorious praying.) As God answers the above prayer for you, the following blessings will flow into your life:

1. Your knowledge of the love of God will become more complete.

2. You will be filled with the knowledge of His will.

3. All wisdom and spiritual understanding will be yours.

4. You will walk worthy of the Lord.

5. You will be pleasing to the Lord in every area of your life.

6. You will be fruitful in every good work.

7. Your knowledge of God will grow.

8. You will be strengthened with all might.

9. You will know God's glorious power.

10. Your patience will grow.

11. Greater joy will be your portion.

These are God's clear promises to you. Meditate in His Word. Reach out to Him in faith. Embrace these promises as your own. Claim them and incorporate their liberating truths into your life. God's promises are foundation blocks on which to build your life, your family, and your future.

> *Therefore everyone who hears these words of mine and puts them into practice is like a wise man who built his house on the rock. The rain came down, the streams rose, and the winds blew and beat*

*against that house; yet it did not fall,
because it had its foundation on the rock.
But everyone who hears these words of
mine and does not put them into practice
is like a foolish man who built his house
on sand. The rain came down, the
streams rose, and the winds blew and
beat against that house, and it fell with a
great crash. (Matt. 7:24-27, NIV)*

The rock that Jesus refers to is the Word of
God — His special book of promises, direction,
and truth. This should be the foundation of
your life. Surrender to Him. Obey Him. Put
His Word into practice in your life. Claim His
promises as your own. Then when the rains
and winds and floods assail, you will not fall
because your foundation is secure.

Don't Worry — Be Happy!

Jesus said, "Therefore I tell you, do not
worry about your life, what you will eat or
drink; or about your body, what you will wear.
Is not life more important than food, and the
body more important than clothes? Look at
the birds of the air; they do not sow or reap or
store away in barns, and yet your heavenly
Father feeds them. Are you not much more
valuable than they? Who of you by worrying
can add a single hour to his life? And why do
you worry about clothes? See how the lilies of

the field grow. They do not labor or spin. Yet I tell you that not even Solomon in all his splendor was dressed like one of these. If that is how God clothes the grass of the field, which is here today and tomorrow is thrown into the fire, will he not much more clothe you, O you of little faith? So do not worry, saying, 'What shall we eat?' or 'What shall we drink?' or 'What shall we wear?' For the pagans run after all these things, and your heavenly Father knows that you need them. But seek first his kingdom and his righteousness, and all these things will be given to you as well. Therefore, do not worry about tomorrow, for tomorrow will worry about itself. Each day has enough trouble of its own" (Matt. 6:25-34, NIV).

God promises to take care of you. He will meet your needs. This certainty is reaffirmed by Paul, "And my God shall supply all your need according to His riches in glory by Christ Jesus" (Phil. 4:19, NKJV). God knows your needs, and He promises to meet each one!

Some people are like the ancient mariner who rises each morning to scan the horizon in search of potential disaster. It seems as if their preoccupation is stuck on "What can I worry about today?" If they don't have something to worry about in the immediate present, they manufacture a concern to focus on. They apparently don't realize that God invites us to

"Cast all your anxiety on him because he cares for you" (1 Pet. 5:7, NIV). They seem to forget Jesus' invitation: "Come to Me, all you who labor and are heavy laden, and I will give you rest" (Matt. 11:28, NKJV).

One reason for much of the worry, stress, strain, and anxiety in our lives comes from failing to believe, remember, heed, or lay our claim to the promises of God. Sometimes the reason for the turmoil we experience can be attributed to not surrendering completely to God or to not obeying Him and His Word. It is amazing how things change when we simply and faithfully do what the Bible says. Remember, God wants you to be happy, and He will never let you down. He promises you rest, happiness, peace, and joy.

Life with God is like living in a flourishing and beautiful kingdom. The land is fertile, productive, peaceful, and beautiful. Ripe, healthy fruits decorate the boughs of every tree. There is shade from the heat, a refreshing river of life, the warmth of God's love, and energizing winds of the Spirit. It is a lush and beautiful land that flows with milk and honey. It is the land of oil and wine. The harvest of the land is bountiful and nutritious. God lives there with you, He speaks to you, and He takes care of your every need.

This is the Promised Land God has created for you. All you have to do is walk through the gate by unlocking it with the promises of God. You will find many of those promises to read and enjoy on the following pages. Envision these promises as fruit on God's tree of blessings. Reach out and pick them, taste them, savor them, enjoy them. Let the nourishment they provide sink deep into your spirit, giving you greater faith, hope, and love. Every promise in the book is yours to claim and keep as you walk closer and closer with the Lord.

Storms Will Come, but the Wise Still Stand

The promises of God are there for us to hold onto and to stand upon in stressful times as well as happy times. Jesus said, "Therefore whoever hears these sayings of Mine, and does them, I will liken him to a wise man who built his house upon the rock" (Matt. 7:24, NKJV). The rock on which to build our lives is the Word of God.

When we hear God's Word, He expects us to do it — to obey it, and to claim His promises even when the times are tough. He wants us to trust Him in both the good times and in the tough times. God's promises strengthen us and enable us to stand when the storms of life assail. It is at such times that the admonition of Ephesians encourages us ". . . that you may be able to withstand in the evil day, and having done all, to stand" (Eph. 6:13, NKJV). We take our stand upon God's Word.

The writer of the Proverbs shows us how this happens: "My son, give attention to my words; incline your ear to my sayings. Do not let them depart from your eyes; Keep them in the midst of your heart; For they are life to those who find them, And health to all their flesh" (Prov. 4:20-22, NKJV).

In fact, it is faith in the promises of God's Word that enables us to keep our hearts with all diligence. We do this by obeying 2 Corinthians 10:5 ". . . bringing every thought into captivity to the obedience of Christ." We want to be careful to protect and guard our heart ". . . for out of it spring the issues of life" (Prov. 4:23, NKJV).

As Jesus pointed out in the Parable of the Sower, the enemy will try to steal the Word of God from our hearts. (See Matt. 13:1-9.) God's Word is the weapon we use to wage successful warfare against the enemy, and the promises of God are penetrating bullets that hit their target every time. The true believer clings to the wisdom of God's Word even when the winds and storms are raging.

The promises of God keep us ". . . steadfast, immovable, always abounding in the work of the Lord" (1 Cor. 15:58, NKJV).

RICH AND PRECIOUS PROMISES

His divine power has given us everything we need for life and godliness through our knowledge of him who called us by his own glory and goodness. Through these he has given us his very great and precious promises, so that through them you may participate in the divine nature and escape the corruption in the world caused by evil desires. (2 Pet. 1:3-4, NIV)

A Cornucopia of Blessings

The promises of God in His Word are numerous. They are great and precious promises that enable you to participate in the divine nature and to escape the corruption in the world that is caused by evil desires. The sheer multitude of God's promises to you is unfathomable, and each promise is so rich that it is unfathomable as well.

In this section of *Believers' Prayers and Promises* I have quoted a select few of God's promises for your spiritual enrichment. Take them one by one, read them, ponder upon them, reflect upon them, and meditate upon them. Let their seeds of faith take root and grow in your heart. The harvest of blessings you will reap will overflow like the fruit that fills a cornucopia.

Select Promises for You

You are saved. "Most assuredly, I say to you, he who believes in Me has everlasting life" (John 6:47, NKJV).

You are justified. "Being justified freely by his grace through the redemption that is in Christ Jesus" (Rom. 3:24).

You are a new creation. "Therefore, if anyone is in Christ, he is a new creation; old things have passed away; behold, all things have become new" (2 Cor. 5:17, NKJV).

You are chosen. "You did not choose Me, but I chose you and appointed you that you should go and bear fruit, and that your fruit should remain" (John 15:16, NKJV).

You are the temple of the Holy Spirit. "Do you not know that your body is the temple of the Holy Spirit who is in you, whom you have received from God, and you are not your own? For you were bought at a price; therefore glorify God in your body and your spirit, which are God's" (1 Cor. 6:19-20, NKJV).

God's benefits are extended to you every day. "Blessed be the Lord, who daily loadeth us with benefits, even the God of our salvation" (Ps. 68:19).

God loves you. "We love him, because he first loved us" (1 John 4:19).

God's love for you is everlasting. "Yes, I have loved you with an everlasting love; therefore with lovingkindness I have drawn you" (Jer. 31:3, NKJV).

Nothing will ever separate you from the love of God. "For I am persuaded that neither death nor life, nor angels nor principalities nor powers, nor things present, nor things to come, nor height nor depth, nor any other created thing, shall be able to separate us from the love of God which is in Christ Jesus our Lord" (Rom. 8:38-39, NKJV).

Perfect peace is available to you. "You will keep him in perfect peace, whose mind is stayed on You, because he trusts in You" (Isa. 26:3, NKJV).

God will give you rest. "Therefore, since a promise remains of entering His rest, let us fear lest any of you seem to have come short of it" (Heb. 4:1, NKJV).

God will give you strength. "The Lord will give strength unto his people; the Lord will bless His people with peace" (Ps. 29:11).

God has forgiven you. "And be kind to one another, tenderhearted, forgiving one another, just as God in Christ forgave you" (Eph. 4:32, NKJV).

Christ lives within you. "To them God willed to make known what are the riches of the glory of this mystery among the Gentiles: which is Christ in you, the hope of glory" (Col. 1:27, NKJV).

You are in Christ. "For as many of you as were baptized into Christ have put on Christ" (Gal. 3:27, NKJV).

You are never alone. "I will never leave you nor forsake you" (Heb. 13:5, NKJV).

You will live forever. "For God so loved the world that He gave His only begotten Son, that whoever believes in Him should not perish but have everlasting life" (John 3:16, NKJV).

You will be safe. "The name of the Lord is a strong tower: the righteous runneth into it, and is safe" (Prov. 18:10).

All your needs will be supplied. "But my God shall supply all your need according to his riches in glory by Christ Jesus" (Phil. 4:19).

Your health will be restored. "For I will restore health to you and heal you of your wounds, says the Lord" (Jer. 30:17, NKJV).

Healing will come. "He sent his word, and healed them" (Ps. 107:20).

You can receive when you pray. "Therefore I say to you, whatever things you ask when you pray, believe that you receive them, and you will have them" (Mark 11:24, NKJV).

You can move mountains. "For assuredly, I say to you, whoever says to this mountain, 'Be removed and be cast into the sea,' and does not doubt in his heart, but believes that those things he says will be done, he will have whatever he says" (Mark 11:23, NKJV).

The joy of the Lord will be your strength. "For the joy of the Lord is your strength" (Neh. 8:10).

God's way is perfect. "As for God, his way is perfect: the word of the Lord is tried: he is a buckler to all those that trust in him" (Ps. 18:30).

God hears your prayer. "Now this is the confidence that we have in Him, that, if we ask anything according to His will, He hears us" (1 John 5:14, NKJV).

The Lord is your Shepherd. "The Lord is my shepherd; I shall not want" (Ps. 23:1).

God's Word will keep you from sin. "Your word I have hidden in my heart, that I might not sin against You" (Ps. 119:11, NKJV).

Heaven is your home. "Surely goodness and mercy shall follow me all the days of my life: and I will dwell in the house of the Lord for ever" (Ps. 23:6).

God will reward your faith. "But without faith it is impossible to please him; for he that cometh to God must believe that he is, and that he is a rewarder of them that diligently seek him" (Heb. 11:6).

God wants you to prosper. "Beloved, I pray that you may prosper in all things and be in health, just as your soul prospers" (3 John 2, NKJV).

The Lord takes pleasure in you. "The Lord takes pleasure in those who fear Him, In those who hope in His mercy" (Ps. 147:11, NKJV).

You can overcome the world. "For whatever is born of God overcomes the world. And this is the victory that has overcome the world — our faith" (1 John 5:4, NKJV).

God will continue His work in your life. "Being confident of this very thing, that he which hath begun a good work in you will perform it until the day of Jesus Christ" (Phil. 1:6).

You will flourish. "The righteous shall flourish like the palm tree: he shall grow like a cedar in Lebanon" (Ps. 92:12).

You will never need to be ashamed. "Be diligent to present yourself approved to God, a worker who does not need to be ashamed, rightly dividing the word of truth" (2 Tim. 2:15, NKJV).

All things are possible to you. "If you can believe, all things are possible to him who believes" (Mark 9:23, NKJV).

God's Word will guide you. "Thy word is a lamp unto my feet, and a light unto my path" (Ps. 119:105).

God will order your steps. "The steps of a good man are ordered by the Lord; And He delights in his way" (Ps. 37:23, NKJV).

God is faithful in fulfilling all His promises. "Let us hold fast the profession of our faith without wavering; (for he is faithful that promised;)" (Heb. 10:23).

A crown of life is reserved for you. "Blessed is the man who endures temptation; for when he has been approved, he will receive the crown of life which God has promised to those who love him" (James 1:12, NKJV).

All things are working together for good in your life. "And we know that all things work together for good to those who love God, to those who are the called according to His purpose" (Rom. 8:28, NKJV).

Your strength will be renewed. "But they that wait upon the Lord shall renew their strength; they shall mount up with wings as eagles; they shall run, and not be weary; and they shall walk, and not faint" (Isa. 40:31).

Your faith will grow. "So then faith comes by hearing, and hearing by the word of God" (Rom. 10:17, NKJV).

God cares. "Casting all your care upon him; for he careth for you" (1 Pet. 5:7).

God will help you. "Fear not, for I am with you; be not dismayed, for I am your God. I will strengthen you, yes, I will help you, I will uphold you with My righteous right hand" (Isa. 41:10, NKJV).

Nothing will be able to offend you. "Great peace have they which love thy law: and nothing shall offend them" (Ps. 119:165).

Everlasting joy will be your portion. "So the ransomed of the Lord shall return, and come to Zion with singing, with everlasting joy on their heads" (Isa. 51:11, NKJV).

Your patience will be rewarded. "That you do not become sluggish, but imitate those who through faith and patience inherit the promises." (Heb. 6:12, NKJV).

No evil will befall you. "No evil shall befall you, nor shall any plague come near your dwelling" (Ps. 91:10, NKJV).

Angels are watching over you. "For he shall give His angels charge over you, to keep you in all your ways. In their hands they shall bear you up, lest you dash your foot against a stone" (Ps. 91:11-12, NKJV).

The infinite riches of God's grace and love are truly immeasurable. These promises from your heavenly Father are a reward for your faith and obedience. I have listed only a few of the promises of His Word to help you see how much God does, in fact, love you. The beautiful part is that His promises are truly limitless. I've only touched the surface of this subject in this chapter.

> *Now to Him who is able to do exceedingly abundantly above all that we ask or think, according to the power that works in us, to him be glory in the church by Christ Jesus to all generations, forever and ever. Amen. (Eph. 3:20-21, NKJV)*

CONQUERING THE IMPOSSIBLE

In all these things we are more than conquerors through him that loved us. (Rom. 8:37)

All Things Are Possible

Jesus said, "All things are possible to him who believes" (Mark 9:23, NKJV). This is His promise to us. He also promised, "Most assuredly, I say to you, he who believes in Me, the works that I do he will do also; and greater works than these he will do, because I go to My Father" (John 14:12, NKJV). The natural mind protests, "But Jesus healed the sick, He raised the dead, He overcame all obstacles. How can we do greater things than these?"

The key, our Master tells us, is *faith*. "But without faith it is impossible to please Him, for he who comes to God must believe that He is, and that He is a rewarder of those who diligently seek Him" (Heb. 11:6, NKJV). Faith is the hand that reaches out to receive all God has. It is faith that pleases God, and it is faith that appropriates His promises.

Is it possible for a person who is terminally ill with cancer or AIDS to be healed? Is it possible for a barren woman to bear a child? Is it possible for a sea to be divided? Is it possible for the dead to be raised to life? Is it possible for a homosexual to become a heterosexual? Is it possible for a fallen soul to be restored? Is it possible for a marriage to be healed?

The world answers each of these questions with a resounding NO because people in the world believe that these things are impossible. The Christian, on the other hand, answers each question with an emphatic YES because our Lord and Master says, "For assuredly, I say to you, if you have faith as a mustard seed, you will say to this mountain, 'Move from here to there,' and it will move; and nothing will be impossible for you" (Matt. 17:20, NKJV).

Faith Sees Clearly

"Now faith is the substance of things hoped for, the evidence of things not seen" (Heb. 11:1). Faith sees beyond the presumed impossibilities, into the realm of spiritual truth and power. It focuses on the promises of God instead of the problems at hand. It envisions the hand of God moving in response to faith. It magnifies God.

Abraham and Sarah were almost 100 years old when two angels came to visit them. The couple extended the traditional Middle Eastern hospitality to their guests, and after they had feasted on veal, bread, and cakes that

Sarah fixed for them, the divine messengers announced, "Sarah will have a son." The prophecy stunned the aged couple and Sarah laughed hysterically. She could not see into the infinite possibilities of God at that moment. Her mind questioned, "How can Abraham and I even have sexual relations at our advanced age? How can my barren womb become fruitful?"

The Lord's reprimand was firm and clear: "Is anything too hard for the Lord?" (Gen. 18:14). It was a rhetorical question (one that does not require an answer because the answer is already obvious). Nothing — absolutely nothing — is too hard for God.

Faith Speaks With Certainty

"The word is near you, in your mouth and in your heart (that is, the word of faith which we preach)" (Rom. 10:8, NKJV). First we see the promise as it is revealed by the Word of God. This is an inner sight — insight, revelation, enlightenment. Then we speak it forth. We believe it in our heart and proclaim it with our mouth: "This is God's special promise to *me*."

Faith builds in our hearts as we speak God's Word: "So then faith comes by hearing, and hearing by the word of God" (Rom. 10:17, NKJV). We need to hear God's Word in our hearts and say it with our mouths. We need to change the sentences we say to ourselves, conforming them to the principles and promises of the Scriptures.

Exchange the ideas of this world with the truths of God's Word. Speak the Word of God to your heart and mind. This is the process that extinguishes doubt. We live in an age of uncertainty and anxiety, but faith speaks peace to our hearts.

When a situation you face seems hopeless say, "I can do all things through Christ who strengthens me" (Phil. 4:13, NKJV). When others say, "It's impossible," tell them, "With men this is impossible, but with God all things are possible" (Matt. 19:26, NKJV).

When the devil tempts you with an evil suggestion, come back at him with God's words, "No temptation has overtaken me except what is common to man. But God is faithful; he will not let me be tempted beyond what I can bear. But when I am tempted, He will also provide a way of escape so that I can bear it" (1 Cor. 10:13, NKJV, personalized).

When fear threatens to overtake you, speak the Word of faith: "For God hath not given us [me] the spirit of fear; but of power, and of love, and of a sound mind" (2 Tim. 1:7).

Faith Hears the Truth

When Abraham heard the angels' announcement he simply believed God. He listened with the ears of faith. Sarah laughed but Abraham heard God, and God rewarded his faith.

"And being not weak in faith, he considered not his own body now dead, when he was about an hundred years old, neither yet the deadness of Sarah's womb; He staggered not at the promise of God through unbelief; but was strong in faith, giving glory to God; And being fully persuaded that, what he had promised, he was able also to perform, And therefore it was imputed to him for righteousness" (Rom. 4:19-22).

Abraham believed God. He believed in hope. God had promised him that he would become the father of many nations. He saw the vision by faith. He spoke the truth of God's Word. He was strong in faith. He took God at His Word. ". . . before him whom he believed, even God, who quickeneth the dead, and calleth those things which be not as though they were" (Rom. 4:17).

Abraham had heard God. He could not be dissuaded by the way things looked in the natural realm. He saw beyond the natural. Through faith, he penetrated the realms of seemingly impossible realities. He seized

God's promise and ran with it. Even though the circumstances made God's promise seem unlikely — even impossible — Abraham called "those things which be not as though they were."

When Abraham was ninety-nine years old, God told him, "I am Almighty God; walk before Me, and be blameless. And I will make My covenant between Me and you, and will multiply you exceedingly . . . for I have made you a father of many nations. I will make you exceedingly fruitful; and I will make nations of you, and kings shall come from you" (Gen. 17:1-6, NKJV). These were the words Abraham, the patriarch of our faith, listened to. He didn't listen to the doubt expressed by his wife. He didn't try to figure it out. He listened to God's words and faith rose in his heart.

Hear the Word of God. Focus on God's promises. Give life to His promises as you speak them forth. Listen to God's words instead of the devil's lies.

Faith Gains the Victory

"For whatsoever is born of God overcometh the world: and this is the victory that overcometh the world, even our faith" (1 John 5:4). How do we conquer the seemingly impossible and overcome the world? Faith is the victory that enables us to be victors instead of victims. We do not have to fail in anything we attempt when we let faith take control of our lives and the circumstances around us.

Doubt keeps us under the circumstances, but faith enables us to rise above them. God has given us a ladder on which to climb above the problems we experience, and the rungs of this ladder are the promises on which He wants us to stand. As we climb, we grow stronger in faith, and we begin to see everything in our lives from a different perspective. The ladder leads us to the heavenly places where we are invited to be seated with Christ: "And hath raised us up together, and made us sit together in heavenly places in Christ Jesus" (Eph. 2:6).

Faith takes control of the circumstances instead of letting the circumstances control us. It joins hands with God who leads us through each difficulty and never lets us down. Faith conquers the impossible by overwhelming it with God's limitless promises and possibilities. In fact, the word *impossibility* is an illusion. It cannot be found in the lexicon of our Lord. There are absolutely no impossibilities in the Kingdom of God.

Faith Stands

"Therefore whoever hears these sayings of Mine, and does them, I will liken him to a wise man who built his house on the rock: and the rain descended, the floods came, and the winds blew and beat on that house; and it did not fall, for it was founded on the rock" (Matt. 7:24-25, NKJV). God wants us to take our stand upon the solid rock of His Word. It is the only firm foundation on which to build our lives.

In hymn sings long ago we used to stand symbolically when we sang:

> Standing on the promises of Christ my King, Thro' eternal ages let His praises ring; Glory in the highest I will shout and sing, Standing on the promises of God.

This faith-filled song was written by R. Kelso Carter in 1886. The second verse effectively reveals the theme of this book:

> Standing on the promises that cannot fail, When the howling storms of doubt and fear assail, By the living Word of God I shall prevail, Standing on the promises of God.

All other ground is sinking sand. Stand with your feet firmly planted on the rock of

God's Word — a book of promises from the Father to you.

Faith Walks

"For we walk by faith, not by sight" (2 Cor. 5:7). The world that is more real than any other is found in the spiritual realm where the sunlight of God's love brightens every day. We will experience the world of the Spirit most fully when we go to heaven. In the meantime, however, as we walk through the kingdom of darkness (this planet), we need to constantly remind ourselves that God's Word gives light in the darkness. "Your word is a lamp to my feet and a light to my path" (Ps. 119:105, NKJV). Our pathway through this shadowy world is paved with the promises and directions of God's Word.

In ancient times travelers who had to continue their journey at night would strap candles to their sandals as they walked along the way. The light provided by the candles would dispell the darkness enough to enable them to avoid holes in the road, scorpions, and poisonous snakes. God's Word is a lamp unto our feet as we make our pilgrimage through this life. It helps us to avoid the pitfalls, potholes, poisonous creatures, and other perils of the journey.

The Word is empowered by the Spirit of God who leads us each step of the way. The Bible is woven together with special promises from God for His children. In fact, the Word of God is more than a Book of promises — it is a promise in and of itself. The Scriptures contain God's covenant-promise to His children. It is this fact more than any other that enables the people of God to walk in faith, not in sight.

Faith Takes Hold

The pages of the Bible present one promise after another. There are promises for mothers, fathers, children, pastors, workers, leaders, believers, dying people, the aged, sick folks, families, teachers, doctors, businesspeople, politicians, policemen, soldiers, worry-warts, evildoers, the righteous, hopeless people, newlyweds, grandparents, gardeners, farmers, liars, missionaries, young people, youth workers, sinners, worshipers, and many others. These promises are contingent on the individual exercise of faith. Faith takes hold of the promises of God, receives them, embraces them, clings to them, speaks them, thanks God for them, and acts upon them.

Faith is an active force in the world today. It can never be passive. It calls for deep personal involvement and commitment. True people of faith are those who continue to believe the promises of God even though all the odds seem to be against them. Theirs is a faith that perseveres. It is willing to pay the price before counting the cost. Faith holds God's hand through the darkest night. Faith counts the blessings instead of the losses. Faith prevails when all else fails.

When we say, "God is faithful," we are actually proclaiming that God is absolutely reliable. We can count on Him to do what He says. This is what faithfulness means, being reliable, loyal, and trustworthy. Do you have unswerving, confident faith that God will be faithful to His Word? Are you full of faith? There is only one way to become a faith-filled believer, and that is by hearing and taking hold of the promises of God that are loudly proclaimed in His Word.

Noah believed God while it was raining and the townspeople laughed. By his faith "he condemned the world and became heir of the righteousness which is according to by faith" (Heb. 11:7, NKJV).

Abraham was called to go to a land he had never heard of before — a land that would eventually become his inheritance. He obeyed God and went, even though he did not know where he was going. "By faith he made his home in the promised land like a stranger in a foreign country" (Heb. 11:9, NIV). Abraham's faith took hold of the promises of God for he was "fully convinced that what He [God] had promised He was also able to perform" (Rom. 4:21, NKJV) In like manner Sarah received strength to conceive "because she judged Him faithful who had promised" (Heb. 11:11, NKJV).

The "Faith Hall of Fame" includes thousands of believers who took God at His Word, taking hold of His promises and acting upon them. By faith Abel offered an appropriate sacrifice to God. By faith Enoch was translated; he never experienced death. By faith Isaac blessed Jacob and Esau. By faith Joshua fought the Battle of Jericho. By faith Moses parted the Red Sea. By faith David slew Goliath, Daniel faced the lions, and all the prophets of God stood upon His promises. By faith Paul faced stonings, shipwrecks, imprisonments, and beatings. By faith Peter healed the lame man. By faith apostles, martyrs, missionaries, and people in all walks of life have taken hold of the promises of God, and in each and every case, God has counted their faith as righteousness, and He has rewarded their faith.

God loves you, as the promises outlined in this book reveal. All you have to do is reach out and take hold of each promise by faith. He will do His part, "For all the promises of God in him [Christ Jesus] are yea, and in him Amen, unto the glory of God by us" (2 Cor. 1:20).

God's special promises for you are weapons in your hands. Use these weapons in faith, and you, like Abraham, Joseph, David, Paul, John, and Peter, will conquer the impossible in your life. The Promised Land (your rightful inheritance) is a place of blessing and infinite possibilities. It is a place where faith becomes reality. *Believers' Prayers and Promises* is designed to lead you into the land of God's promise where the sun keeps on shining, the River of Life keeps on flowing, and the fruits of God's garden keep on growing. It is the best place to be.

WALKING ON THE PROMISES OF GOD

So, we are always confident, knowing that while we are at home in the body we are absent from the Lord. For we walk by faith, not by sight. We are confident, yes, well pleased rather to be absent from the body and to be present with the Lord. (2 Cor. 5:6-8, NKJV)

The Peripatetic Believer

Every believer is on a journey. He or she is a traveler in a foreign country. We are strangers in an alien land because heaven is our true home. While we are finding our way in this world of darkness, we learn that we have to walk by faith, not by sight. God's Word provides us with the light we need for our walk. He gives us a compass that keeps us on track. He holds our hand each step of the way.

A peripatetic person is one who does a lot of walking, hence the subtitle for this section: "The Peripatetic Believer." Faith, as already pointed out, is an active process. It involves both trust and action. This is why the image of walking is often employed to describe a believer's life. God wants us to walk on a walkway that is built from His promises. His promises provide us with steppingstones on which to walk and stand as we walk through life. The road that is built with the promises of God is a "road less traveled," and few there be that find it. The promises of God give us the foundation and guidance we need to find our way. God wants us to walk on His promises.

In this section we will examine some of God's promises in light of the action the believer must take in response to the promises. God's special promises are for us, to be sure, but He expects us to walk in accordance with each promise that He grants. God takes action in our behalf, and He expects us to express our faith in Him by taking corresponding action. This is what James means when he says, ". . . faith without works is dead" (James 2:26). We take our walk on the promises of God. With these thoughts in mind, therefore, let's take a look at some of God's promises that He wants us to walk upon. He gives the promise and He expects us to stand and walk upon it.

Walk in Newness of Life

"Therefore we were buried with Him through baptism into death, that just as Christ was raised from the dead by the glory of the Father, even so we also should walk in newness of life" (Rom. 6:4, NKJV). God gives us a new life when we trust Him for salvation.

It is our responsibility to keep on walking in that newness of life He provides.

Another promise gives us a clear focus on all that this new life entails: "Therefore, if anyone is in Christ, he is a new creation; the old has gone, the new has come!" (2 Cor. 5:17, NIV). We are new creations in Christ Jesus and this enables us to walk in newness of life at all times.

Walk According to the Spirit

We are new creations in Christ Jesus. Therefore, there is now no condemnation for us. (See Rom. 8:1.) We have been set free from all condemnation. In light of these truths, it is necessary for us to "not walk according to the flesh but according to the Spirit" (Rom. 8:4, NKJV). Paul goes on to explain why we must fulfill God's promise by walking according to the Spirit: "For those who live according to the flesh set their minds on the things of the flesh, but those who live according to the Spirit, the things of the Spirit" (Rom. 8:5, NKJV).

Another New Testament promise relates to this one: "I say then: Walk in the Spirit, and you shall not fulfill the lust of the flesh" (Gal. 5:16, NKJV). Notice how this verse puts the action first, followed by God's promise. The promise, in this case, is contingent upon our walk as believers. If we walk according to the Spirit we will not fulfill the lusts of the flesh.

Clearly, our job is to walk according to the Spirit of God.

Walk Honestly

It seems as if the word "honesty" has been redefined in recent times. Certain practices (particularly in the realm of business and politics) that used to be condemnable are now considered commendable. Integrity, in far too many cases, has fallen by the wayside. How is the believer to walk honestly in society today?

"Let us walk honestly, as in the day; not in rioting and drunkenness, not in chambering and wantonness, not in strife and envying. But put ye on the Lord Jesus Christ, and make not provision for the flesh to fulfil the lusts thereof" (Rom. 13:13-14). We walk honestly by putting on the Lord Jesus Christ. We need to be clothed with Him. This promise is similar to the one that is associated with walking in accordance with the Spirit in that by walking honestly, clothed with Christ, we will be certain not to fulfill the lusts of the flesh.

Walk by Faith

As we have seen, receiving God's promises involves more than just passive acquiescence and acceptance. It requires active walking on our part. The renewal of our mind demands that we always walk in newness of life, in accordance with God's promises, His Word, and His Spirit. In order to do so we must exercise faith.

Paul writes, ". . . we walk by faith, not by sight" (2 Cor. 5:7). Those who walk by faith are secure because, ". . . faith is the substance of things hoped for, the evidence of things not seen" (Heb. 11:1). When we walk by faith we don't need evidence in the realm of our five physical senses because we learn and understand with the eyes of our spirit.

Walk in Good Works

God declares, ". . . we are His workmanship, created in Christ Jesus for good works, which God prepared beforehand that we should walk in them" (Eph. 2:10, NKJV). God enables us to do good works, and His promises provide us with the motivation to accomplish them. He promises to continue His workmanship in our lives, and part of that process is to do good works. In fact, this verse declares that good works (fruit-bearing) are what we were created for. God works in our lives so that good works will result.

Walk Worthy of Your Calling

"I, therefore, the prisoner of the Lord, beseech you to walk worthy of the calling with which you were called, with all lowliness and gentleness, with longsuffering, bearing with one another in love, endeavoring to keep the unity of the Spirit in the bond of peace" (Eph. 4:1-3, NKJV).

God gives us His Word and His Spirit in order to enable us to walk worthy before Him in the world. He enables us to walk with all humility, gentleness, patience, love, and diligence. These important qualities of worthiness are related to the fruit of the Spirit that we find listed in Galatians 5:22: "But the fruit of the Spirit is love, joy, peace, longsuffering, kindness, goodness, faithfulness, gentleness, self-control. Against such there is no law" (NKJV).

God has called us out of the world and into His kingdom. We are His representatives on earth. He is continuing His workmanship in our lives so that we will be able to walk worthy of His calling. He promises to fill us with His Spirit so that we will be able to produce the fruit of His Spirit in all the relationships and responsibilities of our lives.

Walk in Jesus Christ

As we examined an earlier promise we discovered that we are to be clothed with Christ. This is possible because of the newness of life that God has promised to all those who receive Jesus Christ as their Savior and Lord. The Bible says, "As you therefore have received Christ Jesus the Lord, so walk in Him, rooted and built up in Him and established in the faith, as you have been taught, abounding in it with thanksgiving" (Col. 2:6-7, NKJV). God promises to root us and build us up in Christ. This will establish us in faith, but our responsibility is to walk in Him and to overflow with gratitude as we do so.

Jesus Christ, our Lord and Savior, is the Word of God in human flesh. "And the Word became flesh and dwelt among us, and we beheld His glory, the glory as of the only begotten of the Father, full of grace and truth" (John 1:14, NKJV). He is the incarnate Word. To walk in Him, therefore, is to abide in His Word. The result will be greater rootedness, edification, establishment, and gratitude in our lives.

Walk Not as Other Gentiles Walk

"This I say, therefore, and testify in the Lord, that you should no longer walk just as the rest of the Gentiles walk, in the futility of their mind, having their understanding darkened, being alienated from the life of God, because of the ignorance that is in them, because of the blindness of their heart; who, being past feeling, have given themselves over to lewdness, to work all uncleanness with greediness. But you have not so learned Christ" (Eph. 4:17-20, NKJV).

God clearly wants our walk to be different from the life-styles of those who are in the world. He wants us to avoid hardness of heart, callousness, sensuality, impurity, and greed. Paul shows us how to walk as we should: ". . . be renewed in the spirit of your mind, and that you put on the new man, which was created according to God, in righteousness and holiness" (Eph. 4:23-24, NKJV).

Walk in Love

Love is the highest law. It is the mark of every true Christian. "Therefore be followers of God as dear children. And walk in love, as Christ also has loved us and given Himself for us, an offering and a sacrifice to God for a sweet-smelling aroma" (Eph. 5:1-2, NKJV). God's promise is that Christ loves you. He gave himself as an offering and sacrifice to God. We receive this promise by faith, but God expects us to walk in love as Christ loved us. Our lives, like His, should be a fragrant aroma in the nostrils of our Father. We must walk in love because, "The only thing that counts is faith expressing itself through love" (Gal. 5:6, NIV).

Walk as Children of Light

Jesus Christ is the Light of the world. (See John 8:12.) He expects us to be the same. "You are the light of the world. A city on a hill cannot be hidden" (Matt. 5:14, NIV). Our natural habitat is the Kingdom of Light, and our role is to walk as children of the light. "For you were once darkness, but now you are light in the Lord. Walk as children of light (for the fruit of the Spirit is in all goodness, righteousness, and truth), finding out what is acceptable to the Lord" (Eph. 5:8-10, NKJV). Paul makes it quite clear in this passage that one of our primary goals as believers is to be pleasing to the Lord. We do this by walking as children of light, avoiding all aspects of darkness in our lives. This implies honesty, as we have already discussed, brightness and radiance, goodness, righteousness, and truth.

The properties of light include purity, dispelling the darkness, warmth, energy, and radiance. We are children of the light; therefore, our walk should reflect each of these qualities. As God's light shines in the darkness, so should we.

Walk Circumspectly (Carefully)

As we continue our walk on the promises of God, we need to exercise caution and care, as Paul points out, "See then that you walk circumspectly, not as fools but as wise, redeeming the time, because the days are evil" (Eph. 5:15-16, NKJV). It has been said that whenever we see the word *therefore* in the Bible we should look to see what it is there for.

The verse preceding this one proclaims, "Awake, you who sleep, arise from the dead, And Christ will give you light" (Eph. 5:14, NKJV). Christ, as pointed out in the preceding section, is the Light of the world. As His light shines upon us and within us we are able to walk circumspectly in this world of darkness. God wants us to walk in wisdom. He wants us to make the most of our time because the days are evil. We do this by walking carefully and wisely upon His sacred promises.

Walk in Wisdom

"Walk in wisdom toward them that are without, redeeming the time" (Col. 4:5). This verse is closely related to the idea of walking circumspectly in that a person who is walking in wisdom will walk carefully because he or she realizes that the times are evil. We are commanded to redeem the time by walking in

wisdom toward those who are outside of
Christ. This means that we are to make the
most of the time that has been given to us.

God promises wisdom to us: "If any of
you lacks wisdom, he should ask God, who
gives generously to all without finding fault,
and it will be given to him. But when he asks,
he must believe and not doubt, because he
who doubts is like a wave of the sea, blown
and tossed by the wind. That man should not
think he will receive anything from the Lord;
he is a double-minded man, unstable in all he
does" (James 1:5-8, NIV).

We need to walk in wisdom and God
promises this to us if we will simply ask Him for
it in faith. The fear of the Lord is the beginning
of wisdom in our lives. (See Ps. 111:10.)

Walk Worthy of God

We are commanded to, ". . . walk worthy
of God who calls you into His own kingdom
and glory" (1 Thess. 2:12, NKJV). God equips
those He calls to do the work He has called
them to do. His Word and His Spirit give us
the faith, the power, and the grace we need to
walk worthy of Him. He promises us His
kingdom and His glory if we will walk in a
manner worthy of Him. We walk in His righteousness and goodness, not our own.

Walk and Please God

In all that we say, think, and do, our focus should be on pleasing God. We please Him most through trust and obedience. He promises so much to us if we will walk in a way that pleases Him. "Finally then, brethren, we urge and exhort you in the Lord Jesus that you should abound more and more, just as you received from us how you ought to walk and to please God" (1 Thess. 4:1, NKJV). The Bible is our instruction manual; it shows us how we ought to walk in order to please God. The Word of God is a book of His covenant with us, and our responsibility is to walk upon each of the promises that form His eternal covenant.

Walk in Truth

"I rejoiced greatly that I have found some of your children walking in truth . . ." (2 John 4, NKJV). God promises that the truth will abide in us and be with us forever. (See 2 John 2.) We know that Jesus Christ is the Truth, and that His Word is truth. His promise is, "Then you will know the truth, and the truth will set you free" (John 8:32, NIV). God wants us to walk in the truth of that freedom, because ". . . if the Son sets you free, you will be free indeed" (John 8:36, NIV).

Walk According to His Commandments

Trusting God's promises involves walking according to His commandments. This is His specific command to us: "This is love, that we walk according to His commandments. This is the commandment, that as you have heard from the beginning, you should walk in it" (2 John 6, NKJV). Notice the connection between obedience and love in this passage. The commandment we need to follow most of all is the Great Commandment, the Love Commandment that Jesus elucidates in Matthew 22:37-39: "Love the Lord your God with all your heart and with all your soul and with all your mind. This is the first and greatest commandment. And the second is like it: 'Love your neighbor as yourself.' All the Law and the Prophets hang on these two commandments" (NIV).

God gives us the commandments and the promises because He loves us. The only appropriate response to such great love is love. True love strives to please the one it adores. This is a good working definition of walking according to the commandments of God.

Walk in the Fear of the Lord

The fear of the Lord is an expression that connotes respect, honor, reverence, awe, and trust. True fear of God transcends any feeling of terror or fright because it leads us to wisdom, knowledge, and trust. It is the fear of God that helps us walk on His promises. God wants us to walk in reverential awe of Him because He knows this will lead us into security, peace, confidence, and true worship.

"Then had the churches rest throughout all Judaea and Galilee and Samaria, and were edified; and walking in the fear of the Lord, and in the comfort of the Holy Ghost . . ." (Acts 9:31). Isn't it interesting that walking in the fear of the Lord and the comfort of the Holy Ghost are connected? This is God's promise to those who walk in reverential fear of Him — rest, edification, and the comfort of the Holy Spirit.

God promises to give you everything you need to walk according to His will. He expects you to walk:

> In newness of life.
> According to the Spirit.
> Honestly.
> By Faith, Not by Sight.
> In Good Works.
> Worthy of His Calling.
> In Jesus Christ.
> Not as Other Gentiles Walk.
> In Love.
> As Children of Light.
> Circumspectly.

In Wisdom.
Worthy of Him.
In a Manner That Pleases Him.
In Truth.
According to His Commandments.
In the Fear of the Lord.

The ability to demonstrate these qualities in life is found in the promises of God which are outlined in meditation form on the following pages. God does not expect more from you than what He promises to provide for you. His strength, righteousness, power, love, wisdom, and truth are part and parcel of His special promises to you. Trust His promises and then try your best. Leave the rest to God.

In the pages that follow, many Bible promises have been arranged under specific topics for your spiritual growth and edification. Every time a promise from the Word of God is used it is footnoted so that you will have an easy reference to follow for further study of the topic.

I believe that you will be thrilled by the sheer multitude of God's special promises to you. The promises have been personalized so that you will be able to apply each one to your life and situation. In so doing I pray that you will personally receive and experience the power of God's promises to you.

1

CHRIST IS MY ABODE

Bible Promise: "I am the vine, you are the branches; He who abides in Me, and I in him, bears much fruit; for without Me you can do nothing" (John 15:5, NKJV).

Bible Meditation: I choose to make the Lord Jesus Christ my abode.[1] I will abide in Him.[2] He is the true vine, and my heavenly Father is the vinedresser.[3] His Word has brought cleansing to me,[4] and it has renewed my mind.[5] Jesus abides in me, and I abide in Him.[6] Because the Lord has grafted me into the vine of life,[7] I am able to bear much fruit.[8] The Father prunes me and trims me so that I will be even more fruitful,[9] and I am grateful for His pruning in my life.

I will continue to abide in Jesus and to let His words abide in me. By so doing I can be certain that whatever I ask in accordance with His will shall be done.[10] The end result will be that the Father will be glorified, I will be fruitful, and these things will show that I am a true disciple of Jesus Christ.[11] I will abide in Jesus' great love for me.[12] Another result of my abiding in Christ will be that when He returns to earth, I will have confidence and not be ashamed before Him.[13]

It is my desire to follow in the footsteps of my Master.[14] Because I abide in Him I realize that I need to walk in the same way that He walked.[15] In Jesus Christ I live and move and have my being.[16] I am in Him,[17] and He is in me.[18]

God's Word declares that if anyone does not abide in Jesus, he or she will be thrown away as a branch and he or she will dry up. Jesus has chosen me to bear much fruit,[19] and by abiding in Him, and with His words abiding in me, I will be a fruit-bearing Christian each and every day.

My Lord and Master prayed that I would be one with my brothers and sisters in Him.[20] He said that as He and the Father are one, so would believers be with each other.[21] As I learn how to be one with my brothers and sisters, and with Him, the world will believe in Jesus Christ.[22]

References: (1) John 15:4; (2) John 15:7; (3) John 15:1; (4) John 15:3; (5) Romans 12:2; (6) John 15:5; (7) Romans 11:23; (8) John 15:5; (9) John 15:2; (10) John 15:7; (11) John 15:8; (12) John 15:10; (13) 1 John 2:28; (14) 1 Peter 2:21; (15) 1 John 2:3-6; (16) Acts 17:28; (17) 1 John 3:24; (18) Colossians 1:27; (19) John 15:16; (20) John 17:21; (21) John 17:21; (22) John 17:21.

Bible Prayer: Lord,[1] thank you for the life that flows through the True Vine which is Jesus Christ.[2] All authority in heaven and in earth has been given Him,[3] and He has chosen to take up His residence in me.[4] I am His abode,[5] and I always want to abide in Him.[6] Thank you for calling me to be a fruit-bearing Christian, Lord,[7] and for giving me the means to bear fruit for you by abiding in you and letting your words abide in me.[8] It is always my desire to glorify you.[9] In Jesus' name I pray,[10] Amen.

References: (1) *Jude 4; (2) John 15:1; (3) Matthew 28:18; (4) Revelation 3:20; (5) Colossians 1:27; (6) John 15:4; (7) John 15:16; (8) John 15:7; (9) John 15:8; (10) John 15:16.*

Related Scriptures: *Psalms 61:7; Psalms 91:1; Luke 24:29; John 12:46; John 14:16; John 15:10; 1 John 2:27; 1 John 2:28.*

ABUNDANCE

2

ABUNDANT LIFE IS MINE

Bible Promise: "The thief does not come except to steal, and to kill, and to destroy. I have come that they may have life, and that they may have it more abundantly" (John 10:10, NKJV).

Bible Meditation: God is the Father of lights with whom there is no variation or shadow of turning.[1] He is the Giver of every good and perfect gift,[2] and He wants me to enjoy abundant life in the here-and-now. Jesus came to give me abundant life.[3]

I receive His promise of abundant living. I claim it as my own. He wants me to experience fullness,[4] wholeness,[5] and abundance in every area of my life. Living with Jesus is an abundant life that gives me unspeakable joy and inexpressible glory.[6] My heart is thankful in the certainty that God, my loving Father,[7] wants me to prosper and enjoy good health.[8]

The infilling presence of His Spirit gives life to my body and strength to my soul.[9] He is granting prosperity to me.[10] He blesses me with an abundance of provisions.[11] In fact, His blessings literally rain upon me, and they are so numerous that I feel sure that I will not be able to contain them all.[12] God has opened the very windows of heaven in order to pour out His abundance upon me and my loved ones.[13]

The Lord supplies all my needs according to His riches in glory.[14] I celebrate His goodness to me.[15] I bask in His presence as I willingly accept all the good gifts coming from His hands.[16]

There is never a need for me to worry.[17] God cares for me.[18] He wants to give me everything I need.[19] He will do so.[20] He is the Bread of life,[21] and as He supplied manna for His children in the wilderness,[22] so will He provide me with my daily bread.[23] He is meeting every need of my soul, spirit, and body.[24] He has brought me into a place of abundance,[25] and I will never have to want again.[26]

God is giving me the desires of my heart.[27] He delights in doing so many wonderful things for me.[28] I will always give top priority to seeking Him and His righteousness, happily realizing that as I do so, He will meet all my needs.[29] Therefore, I cast all my cares upon Him.[30]

Life consists of so much more than the abundance of possessions.[31] Godliness with contentment is greater gain than many riches.[32] The greatest form of abundance that God provides is spiritual abundance. In His great love for me, the Lord has given me abundant life in every dimension, and as I reflect on the abundance I enjoy in every area of my life, praise wells up from my inner depths.[33]

References: (1) James 1:17; (2) James 1:17; (3) John 10:10; (4) John 1:16; (5) Mark 5:34; (6) 1 Peter 1:8; (7) 2 Corinthians 1:2; (8) 3 John 2; (9) Romans 8:11; (10) Psalms 35:27; (11) Nehemiah 2:20; (12) Malachi 3:10; (13) Malachi 3:10; (14) Philippians 4:19; (15) Psalms 52:1; (16) John 1:16; (17) Matthew 6:34; (18) 1 Peter 5:7; (19) Luke 12:32; (20) Philippians 4:19; (21) John 6:35; (22) Numbers 11:7; (23) Luke 11:3; (24) Philippians 4:19; (25) 2 Corinthians 9:11; (26) Psalms 23:1; (27) Psalms 37:4; (28) Isaiah 62:4; (29) Philippians 4:19; (30) 1 Peter 5:7; (31) Luke 12:15; (32) 1 Timothy 6:6; (33) Psalms 147:1.

Bible Prayer: Dear Lord,[1] you are my Shepherd.[2] Because of your protective care[3] and supply[4] I will never have to want for anything.[5] You supply all my needs.[6] You are immeasurably great,[7] and you are greatly to be praised.[8] You have given me unsearchable riches to enjoy.[9] I receive the treasures you give to me.[10] Thank you for meeting all my needs.[11] I will walk in the abundant living you provide throughout this day.[12] In Jesus' name I pray,[13] Amen.

References: (1) Exodus 15:2; (2) John 10:11; (3) 1 Peter 5:7; (4) 2 Corinthians 8:9; (5) Deuteronomy 8:9; (6) Philippians 4:19; (7) 1 Chronicles 29:11; (8) Psalms 48:1; (9) Proverbs 8:18; (10) Matthew 6:20; (11) Job 36:11; (12) Isaiah 48:15; (13) John 16:24.

Related Scriptures: *Deuteronomy 28:11; Job 36:31; Psalms 23; Psalms 66:12; Psalms 118:24; Psalms 122:7; Psalms 132:15-16; Matthew 13:12; Matthew 25:29; Romans 5:17; 2 Corinthians 8:2.*

AMBASSADOR

3

I AM THE LORD'S
AMBASSADOR

Highest Rank (handwritten)

Bible Promise: "Now then, we are ambassadors for Christ, as though God were pleading through us; we implore you on Christ's behalf, be reconciled to God. For He made Him who knew no sin to be sin for us, that we might become the righteousness of God in Him" (2 Cor. 5:20-21, NKJV).

Bible Meditation: It is a privilege for me to be the Lord's ambassador.[1] He is the Light of the world,[2] and He has called me to be a light in the world as well.[3] I will let His light so shine before others that they will glorify my Father who is in heaven.[4] Jesus has said that I am also the salt of the earth,[5] and realizing that one of the properties of salt is to produce thirst, I want to live my life in such a way that others will become thirsty for Jesus and will want to taste and see that the Lord is good.[6]

As a witness for the Lord Jesus Christ,[7] I will lead others to the rivers of living water[8] so that they will be able to drink from the water of life freely.[9] When they drink this water they shall never thirst again.[10]

Realizing my responsibility as the Lord's ambassador, I will sanctify the Lord God in my heart and be ready to give an answer to anyone who asks me, a reason for the hope that I have within my heart. I will always endeavor to share this good news with meekness and love.[11] I will study to show myself approved unto God, a workman that never needs to be ashamed because I have learned how to divide and share his Word in the right way.[12] I will walk in love so that all will know that I am a disciple of the Lord Jesus Christ.[13]

The Bible says that a soul-winner is a wise person,[14] and I want always to be a wise ambassador of my Lord, one who wins souls for His kingdom. God's Spirit continuously fills me with the power I need to be an effective witness for my Lord,[15] and I will let His Spirit lead me to the people He wants me to reach.[16] I will obey my Lord's command and go forth into the world, preaching the Gospel of Jesus Christ wherever I go.[17]

References: (1) Ephesians 6:20; (2) John 1:9; (3) Matthew 5:14; (4) Matthew 5:16; (5) Matthew 5:13; (6) Psalms 34:8; (7) Acts 1:8; (8) John 7:38; (9) John 4:11; (10) John 4:13-14; (11) 1 Peter 3:15; (12) 2 Timothy 2:15; (13) John 13:35; (14) Proverbs 11:30; (15) Acts 1:8; (16) Romans 8:14; (17) Mark 16:15.

Bible Prayer: God,[1] I will never be ashamed of the testimony of my Lord and Savior, Jesus Christ.[2] The Gospel of Christ is your power unto salvation to all who will believe.[3] Through Him, you have saved me, and called me with a holy calling.[4] I thank you that you have called me to be your ambassador.[5] I know this calling has come to me not because of my own works, but because of your own purpose and grace in my life.[6] Help me, Lord, to be faithful in preaching the Word, to be instant in season and out of season, to reprove, rebuke, and exhort with all longsuffering and doctrine.[7] In Jesus' name I pray,[8] Amen.

References: (1) *Genesis 1:1;* (2) *2 Timothy 1:8;* (3) *Romans 1:16;* (4) *2 Timothy 1:9;* (5) *2 Corinthians 5:20;* (6) *2 Timothy 1:9;* (7) *2 Timothy 4:2;* (8) *John 15:16.*

Related Scriptures: *Luke 6:45; Luke 12:8-9; John 13:35; Psalms 26:7; Psalms 104:33.*

4

GUARDIAN ANGELS ARE PROTECTING ME

Bible Promise: "The angel of the Lord encamps all around those who fear Him, and delivers them" (Ps. 34:7, NKJV).

Bible Meditation: God assigns His angels to protect me and my loved ones.[1] He gives His angels charge over me, to keep my feet from stumbling.[2] The angels engage in spiritual warfare in my behalf, warring against the fallen angels who are ruled by Satan.[3] God's angels form an hedge of protection around me and my loved ones.[4]

God commands His angels to take action in my behalf, directing them to guard me in all my ways.[5] They will lift me up in their hands so that I will not fall.[6] The Lord loves me and He wants to protect me.[7]

The angelic host are a part of the great cloud of witnesses that encourages me to keep on running the race that is set before me with patience as I look unto Jesus who is the Author and Finisher of my faith.[8] These angel-protectors hearken to God's Word when I speak it in faith, and they take action to bring it to pass.[9]

In the spiritual realm there are thousands of chariots and tens of thousands of angels.[10] It thrills me to realize that this innumerable company of angels is working in my behalf.[11] The angels of heaven are sent by my Father to serve me in an effort to assure that my inheritance of His salvation will remain secure.[12]

The angels praise and worship God;[13] I choose to be like them in this. If they bring messages from my Father to me, I will receive their words of warning and counsel.[14] They help to fulfill God's provision and will in my life; I accept their care.[15] They protect me; I feel secure.[16] They care for me; I sense their nurturing presence.[17] The knowledge of God's angelic protection fills me with His love and peace.

I will walk in confidence, knowing that the angels are watching over me and helping me each step of the way.

References: (1) *Psalms 91:11;* (2) *Psalms 91:12;* (3) *Hebrews 1:14;* (4) *Job 1:10;* (5) *Luke 4:10;* (6) *Luke 4:11;* (7) *Proverbs 18:10;* (8) *Hebrews 12:1-2;* (9) *Psalms 103:20;* (10) *Psalms 68:17;* (11) *Hebrews 12:22;* (12) *Hebrews 1:14;* (13) *Revelation 22:8-9;* (14) *Luke 1:26-38;* (15) *Matthew 18:10;* (16) *Daniel 6:16-23;* (17) *Matthew 4:11.*

Bible Prayer: Eternal God,[1] how I praise you for the angels you send to protect me,[2] warn me,[3] provide for me,[4] and care for me.[5] I receive their loving help in my life, and as I do so, I feel secure and happy. Thank you for angels, Father. I look forward to meeting the angels you have assigned to my care when I join the family of God in heaven.[6] In Jesus' name I pray,[7] Amen.

References: *(1) Deuteronomy 33:27; (2) Psalms 91:11-12; (3) Psalms 34:7; (4) Hebrews 12:22; (5) Hebrews 1:14; (6) Matthew 25:31; (7) John 16:23.*

Related Scriptures: *Genesis 16:7; Exodus 23:20-23; Nehemiah 9:6; Job 1:6-12; Psalms 91:11; Matthew 18:10; Luke 1:26; Luke 4:10; Acts 12:15; Hebrews 1:7.*

ANOINTED

5

I AM ANOINTED

Bible Promise: "You prepare a table before me in the presence of my enemies. You anoint my head with oil; my cup overflows" (Ps. 23:5, NIV).

Bible Meditation: The Anointed One is Jesus Christ,[1] and He has chosen to dwell within me by His Spirit.[2] All power in heaven and on earth reside in Him,[3] and now He lives in me.[4] Therefore, all power is in me — miracle-working power through His Spirit.[5]

I can do all things through Christ Jesus, my Lord.[6] He promises me that I will be able to accomplish even greater things than He did[7] through the anointing of His Spirit that is within me and upon me.[8] Jesus said that His ascension to heaven was expedient for me[9] because it was through His ascension that He was able to send His Spirit to give me strength through the anointing.[10]

My head is anointed with the oil of the Holy Spirit.[11] My hands and feet and eyes are anointed as well.[12] Truly, my cup overflows with this anointing through which others will receive healing, salvation, and other miracles.[13] I desire to become God's extended hands, reaching out to all those who are oppressed by the enemy.[14]

My anointing comes from the Anointed One, the Messiah, Christ Jesus, who empowers me.[15] What I am able to accomplish does not come through human might, power, or ability, but through His Spirit.[16] God anointed Jesus of Nazareth with the Holy Spirit and with fire[17] so that He would be empowered to go forth doing good and healing all who were oppressed by the devil.[18] Through Him, that same anointing is my portion today.

This is my calling — to preach the good news to the poor, to proclaim freedom to those who are in bondage, to give sight to the blind, to bind up the broken-hearted, and to release the oppressed.[19] In fact, I have an unction from the Holy One[20] that equips me to fulfill this calling.

My anointing is a blessing beyond description. It is joy unspeakable and full of glory.[21] I have been anointed with the oil of joy,[22] and this joy is my strength.[23] It is a miraculous anointing that breaks every burden, destroys every yoke, and truly sets me free.[24] I receive and enjoy this anointing in my life today.

References: (1) Luke 4:18; (2) Acts 1:8; (3) Matthew 28:18; (4) Colossians 1:27; (5) Romans 8:11; (6) Philippians 4:13; (7) John 14:12; (8) 1 John 2:20; (9) John 16:7; (10) John 14:16-18; (11) Psalms 23:5;

(12) Acts 14:3; (13) Mark 16:17-18; (14) Acts 10:38; (15) Colossians 3:17; (16) Colossians 1:11; (17) Luke 3:16; (18) Acts 10:38; (19) Isaiah 61:1; (20) 1 John 2:20; (21) 1 Peter 1:8; (22) Hebrews 1:9; (23) Nehemiah 8:10; (24) Nahum 1:13.

Bible Prayer: Dear God in heaven,[1] I praise you for the anointing of your Holy Spirit that empowers me[2] to minister to others in your matchless name.[3] You anoint my head with oil[4] that provides me and others with joy, healing, and freedom.[5] Thank you, Lord. I receive your anointing today. It is within me[6] and it is on me.[7] It empowers me to live in total victory[8] and to walk in faith.[9] Thank you for your wonderful anointing. In Jesus' name I pray,[10] Amen.

References: (1) Luke 11:2; (2) Acts 1:8; (3) Colossians 3:17; (4) Psalms 23:5; (5) Isaiah 61:3; (6) 1 John 2:27; (7) Isaiah 61:1; (8) 1 Corinthians 15:57; (9) 2 Corinthians 5:7; (10) John 15:16.

Related Scriptures: 1 Chronicles 16:22; Psalms 45:7; Luke 4:18; Acts 10:38; 2 Corinthians 1:21.

6

JESUS HAS GIVEN ME AUTHORITY

Bible Promise: "All authority has been given to Me in heaven and on earth. Go therefore and make disciples of all the nations, baptizing them in the name of the Father and of the Son and of the Holy Spirit, teaching them to observe all things that I have commanded you; and lo, I am with you always, even to the end of the age" (Matt. 28:18-20, NKJV).

Bible Meditation: The Lord Jesus Christ has commissioned me to teach in His name,[1] to take authority over the enemy,[2] to do His works,[3] to set the captives free,[4] and to subdue the earth.[5] He has all authority in heaven and on earth,[6] and He lives within me.[7] Therefore, all authority in heaven and on earth dwells within me; indeed, I can do all things through Christ who strengthens me.[8]

The power of His name,[9] the power of His blood,[10] the power of the Holy Spirit,[11] and the power of His Word[12] are with me at all times. Greater is He that is in me than he that is in the world.[13] Whatever I ask in the name of Jesus shall be granted.[14] The blood of Jesus Christ

cleanses me from all sin.[15] The Holy Spirit
empowers me to live a victorious life.[16]

The Word of God is my weapon in spiritual
warfare; it is the sword of the Spirit.[17] It is
sharper than any two-edged sword.[18] Through
Christ and the Word of God, I am more than a
conqueror.[19] Through the power of the Word,
the name of Jesus Christ, the Holy Spirit, and
the blood of Jesus I am able to take spiritual
authority over the enemy, the works of darkness,
and sin, thus fulfilling God's original intention
for mankind: "Be fruitful and multiply; fill the
earth and subdue it; have dominion over the
fish of the sea, over the birds of the air, and over
every living thing that moves on the earth."[20]

References: (1) *Mark 16:15; (2) Luke 10:19;*
(3) John 14:12; (4) Luke 4:18; (5) Genesis 1:28;
(6) Matthew 28:18; (7) Colossians 1:27; (8) Philippians
4:13; (9) Ephesians 1:20-22; (10) Revelation 12:11;
(11) Acts 1:8; (12) Hebrews 4:12; (13) 1 John 4:4;
(14) John 16:23; (15) 1 John 1:7; (16) Ephesians 6:10;
(17) Ephesians 6:17; (18) Hebrews 4:12; (19) Romans
8:37; (20) Genesis 1:28.

Bible Prayer: O Lord,[1] I thank you for the spiritual authority you have imparted to me
through prayer,[2] your Word,[3] the blood of
Jesus,[4] the indwelling Holy Spirit,[5] and the
name of Jesus Christ.[6] You have given me
power to tread on serpents and scorpions, and

over all the power of the enemy, and as I use the spiritual authority you give to me, I realize that nothing shall by any means hurt me.[7] I choose to walk in that authority throughout this day by clothing myself in your full armor — the helmet of salvation, the girdle of truth, the breastplate of righteousness, the shoes of the gospel of peace, the shield of faith, the sword of the Spirit, and prayer.[8] I know that I can do all things through Christ who strengthens me.[9] Because of the spiritual authority you have imparted to me through faith I am able to accomplish whatever you commission me to do.[10] Strengthen me with might by your Spirit in my inner man now as I pray,[11] in the mighty name of Jesus,[12] Amen.

References: (1) Psalms 143:11; (2) John 14:13; (3) Ephesians 6:17; (4) Revelation 12:11; (5) Romans 8:11; (6) Mark 16:17; (7) Luke 10:19; (8) Ephesians 6:11-20; (9) Philippians 4:13; (10) Matthew 28:18; (11) Ephesians 3:16; (12) John 15:16.

Related Scriptures: James 4:7-8; Psalms 121:7-8; Psalms 91:3-7.

7

I AM BLESSED!

Bible Promise: "Blessed be the God and Father of our Lord Jesus Christ, who has blessed us with every spiritual blessing in the heavenly places in Christ" (Eph. 1:3, NKJV).

Bible Meditation: I am blessed. My God has given me every spiritual blessing in Christ.[1] He chose me in Him before the foundation of the world to be holy and blameless in His sight.[2] In love, He predestined me to be adopted as His child.[3]

In Him I have been redeemed from the hand of the enemy.[4] His blood has set me free.[5] My sins have been forgiven.[6] My Father has lavished the riches of His grace upon me.[7] He has given me spiritual wisdom and understanding.[8] He has even made known to me the mystery of His will according to His good pleasure, which He purposed in Christ.[9]

God has exalted my Lord Jesus Christ and given Him a name that is above every name. My Father has brought all things in heaven and on earth under the Lordship of Christ.[10] I was chosen in Him to be for the praise of His glory, along with all other people who believe in Him.[11]

Because I believe in Him I have been sealed with the promised Holy Spirit who is a deposit that guarantees my inheritance until the redemption of all those who are God's possession.[12]

I am truly blessed. My Father loves me, and I love Him.[13] He gives me His blessing in every part of my life. His blessing brings prosperity,[14] health,[15] victory,[16] and joy[17] to me. To be blessed is to be happy, and as I count my blessings, my heart fills with gladness,[18] joy,[19] and gratitude.[20]

References: (1) *Ephesians 1:3; (2) Ephesians 1:4; (3) Galatians 4:5; (4) Psalms 107:2; (5) 1 John 1:7; (6) 1 John 1:9; (7) Ephesians 2:7; (8) Ephesians 1:18; (9) Ephesians 1:9; (10) Philippians 2:9-10; (11) Ephesians 1:6; (12) Ephesians 1:13; (13) 1 John 4:19: (14) Psalms 1:3; (15) 3 John 2; (16) Isaiah 25:8; (17) 1 John 1:4; (18) Psalms 4:7; (19) Romans 15:13; (20) Colossians 2:7.*

Bible Prayer: Thank you,[1] Father, for blessing me with every spiritual[2] and temporal[3] blessing. You have given me so much, including the spirit of wisdom and revelation that enables me to know you and your ways more fully.[4] You have given me enlightenment that helps me to see and to know the hope to which you have called me.[5] You have bestowed spiritual blessings and riches upon me.[6] I truly am blessed, Lord, and I love you and praise you for your blessing and for all the blessings you have given to me so freely.[7] In Jesus' name I pray,[8] Amen.

References: *(1) Philippians 4:6; (2) Ephesians 1:3; (3) Philippians 4:19; (4) Ephesians 1:17; (5) Ephesians 4:4; (6) Ephesians 3:8; (7) Psalms 129:8; (8) John 16:23.*

Related Scriptures: *Psalms 29:11; Proverbs 10:22; Proverbs 28:20; Isaiah 30:18; Ezekiel 34:26; Matthew 5; Romans 10:12; Ephesians 1; James 1:12.*

8

THERE IS POWER IN THE BLOOD OF JESUS

Bible Promise: "In him we have redemption through his blood, the forgiveness of sins, in accordance with the riches of God's grace that he lavished on us with all wisdom and understanding" (Eph. 1:7-8, NIV).

Bible Meditation: It is the blood of Jesus Christ, through the eternal Spirit, that purges my conscience from dead works to serve the living God.[1] I was not redeemed with corruptible, material things, such as silver and gold, but with the precious blood of Christ — the Lamb of God who is without any blemishes or imperfections.[2] It is through Jesus Christ, who shed His blood for me, that I am able to believe in God, who raised Him from the dead and gave Him glory, so that my faith and hope are in God.[3]

The blood of Jesus Christ is the sacrifice that reconciles me to God, and being reconciled, I will be saved by His life.[4] When the blood was applied to the doorposts of the houses of the Israelites, the plague passed by their dwellings.[5] God promises that, when He sees the blood He will be sure to protect me and my family.[6] I plead the protection of the blood of Jesus Christ over my home and family, and I know God will plant His hedge of protection around us.[7] As for me and my house, we will serve the Lord.[8]

When I walk in the light, as Jesus is in the light, I have fellowship with other believers, and the blood of Jesus Christ cleanses me from all sin.[9] The blood of Jesus Christ was shed for the remission (forgiveness) of my sins.[10] Therefore, I am freely justified by His grace through the redemption provided by the blood of Jesus.[11] He is a propitiation (sacrifice) for my sins, and I respond to this fact with faith in His blood. I will declare His righteousness to the world, and I will accept the certainty that all my sins have been remitted by His blood.[12] In the same way that I have been justified through His blood, I know I shall be saved from wrath through Him.[13]

God, in His foreknowledge, chose me through the sanctification of His Spirit, unto the obedience and sprinkling of the blood of Jesus Christ.[14] Through Jesus' blood I am able to draw near to the Father.[15] There is such great power in His blood which gives me peace and access, by one Spirit, to my Father in heaven.[16]

Though the enemy is the accuser of the brethren, I am able to overcome him through the blood of Jesus Christ and by the word of my testimony.[17]   The God of peace who brought Jesus back from the dead through the blood of His everlasting covenant with me, will make me perfect in every good work to do His will. He will work in me that which is well-pleasing in His sight, through Jesus Christ, to whom be glory forever.[18]

References: *(1) Hebrews 9:14; (2) 1 Peter 1:18-19; (3) 1 Peter 1:20-21; (4) Romans 5:10; (5) Exodus 12:13; (6) Exodus 12:13; (7) Job 1:10; (8) Joshua 24:15; (9) 1 John 1:7; (10) Matthew 26:28; (11) Romans 3:24; (12) Romans 3:25; (13) Romans 5:9; (14) 1 Peter 1:2; (15) Ephesians 2:13; (16) Ephesians 2:18; (17) Revelation 12:11; (18) Hebrews 13:20-21.*

Bible Prayer: Loving God,[1] your covenant with me required that blood be shed for the atonement of my sins.[2]   Thank you for commending your love toward me in that while I was yet a sinner, the Lord Jesus Christ shed His blood for me.[3] Because He did so, I am now justified by His blood, and I know I will be saved from the wrath which is to come.[4] Through Holy Communion you have provided a wonderful means of reminding me that through your grace and my precious Savior's blood I am able to dwell in Him and He in me.[5] Through your Son I have redemption because He shed His blood for me.[6] My sins are forgiven.[7] My future is secure.[8] I have access through prayer to the Father.[9] I have spiritual

victory.[10] My fear is gone.[11] I know God is
near.[12] I know I live in Christ and He lives in
me.[13] Yes, there is power in the blood, Father,
and I thank you again for the precious blood of
Christ.[14] In Jesus' name I pray,[15] Amen.

References: (1) *John 16:27; (2) Leviticus 17:11;
(3) Romans 5:8; (4) Romans 5:9; (5) John 6:56;
(6) Ephesians 1:7; (7) Hebrews 9:22; (8) Romans
5:9; (9) Ephesians 2:18; (10) Revelation 12:11;
(11) Exodus 12:13; (12) Psalms 46:1; (13) John
6:56; (14) Romans 5:8; (15) John 15:16.*

*Related Scriptures: 1 Corinthians 10:16; 1 Corinthians
11:25-27; Hebrews 9:22; Exodus 24:8; Luke 22:19-20.*

9

I AM CALLED

Bible Promise: "As you know how we exhorted, and comforted, and charged every one of you, as a father does his own children, that you would walk worthy of God who calls you into His own kingdom and glory" (1 Thess. 2:11-12, NKJV).

Bible Meditation: God has called me.[1] He has called me to liberty,[2] to be a saint,[3] to peace,[4] to light,[5] and to an intimate, personal relationship with Him.[6] I have been sanctified in Christ Jesus, called to be a saint along with all who call upon the Name of Jesus Christ.[7] God is faithful, and He has called me into the fellowship with His Son, Jesus Christ.[8]

With great thanksgiving in my heart, I realize that Christ is the power of God and the wisdom of God to all whom God calls.[9] I can see my calling.[10] God has chosen the foolish things of the world to confound the wise, and He has chosen the weak things of the world to confound the things which are mighty. He has also chosen the base things of the world, the things which are despised, to bring to nothing things that are.[11]

All things work together for good in my life — in the lives of all who are called according to my Father's purpose.[12] He has called me and He has justified me.[13] He has called me so that He might make known the riches of his glory unto me.[14] I will abide in the calling that God has extended to me.[15] I am called to freedom,[16] to the glorious liberty of the sons of God.[17] I am called to be the Lord's servant,[18] and what a privilege that is for me.

God has called me into the grace of Christ.[19] I have been called into His freedom,[20] and I will not use this liberty as an occasion to the flesh, but through love to serve my Lord and others.[21] This is why I have been called.

I will walk worthy of the vocation to which I have been called.[22] With all lowliness and meekness, with patience and endurance, I will honor others in love.[23] With God's help, I will endeavor to keep the unity of the Spirit in the bond of peace.[24] There is one body, and one Spirit, and I have been called in one hope of my calling.[25] There is one Lord, one faith, one baptism, one God and Father of all, who is above all, and through all, and within me.[26] These are all wonderful aspects of my calling — a calling that gives me a purpose for living.

References: (1) 1 Thessalonians 2:12; (2) Galatians 5:13; (3) Romans 1:7; (4) 1 Corinthians 7:15; (5) 1 Peter 2:9; (6) 1 Corinthians 1:9; (7) 1 Corinthians 1:2; (8) 1 Corinthians 1:9; (9) 1 Corinthians 1:24; (10) 1 Corinthians 1:26; (11) 1 Corinthians 1:27-28; (12) Romans 8:28; (13) Romans 8:30; (14) Romans

9:23; (15) 1 Corinthians 7:20; (16) 1 Corinthians 7:21;
(17) Romans 8:21; (18) 1 Corinthians 7:22;
(19) Galatians 1:15; (20) Galatians 5:13;
(21) Galatians 5:13; (22) Ephesians 4:1; (23) Ephesians
4:2; (24) Ephesians 4:3; (25) Ephesians 4:3;
(26) Ephesians 4:4-6.

Bible Prayer: Heavenly Father,[1] thank you for calling me to be your child.[2] You have called me to be one of your saints.[3] It gives me great peace to know that all things work together for good in my life because I am one of your called ones; you have called me according to your eternal purpose.[4] It is wonderful to realize, Lord, that I am a part of your body on earth[5] — the *ecclesia*, the Church of Jesus Christ[6] — I am no longer my own, but you have bought me,[7] redeemed me,[8] set me free,[9] cleansed me,[10] and delivered me.[11] Understanding your calling in my life motivates me to live righteously[12] and soberly before you.[13] In Jesus' name[14] I pray, Amen.

References: (1) Isaiah 64:8; (2) Romans 8:28;
(3) 1 Corinthians 1:2; (4) Romans 8:28; (5) 1 Corinthians
12:27; (6) Colossians 1:24; (7) 1 Corinthians 6:20;
(8) Zechariah 10:8; (9) Galatians 5:13; (10) 1 John
1:9; (11) 1 Thessalonians 1:10; (12) Titus 2:12;
(13) Romans 12:3; (14) John 15:16.

Related Scriptures: Romans 1:7; Romans 8:30;
Galatians 1:15; Colossians 3:15; 1 Timothy 6:12;
2 Timothy 1:9; 1 Peter 1:15.

C A R E

10

GOD CARES FOR ME

Bible Promise: "Casting all your care on Him, for He cares for you" (1 Pet. 5:7, NKJV).

Bible Meditation: My Father does care about me.[1] He does not want me to be anxious or fearful about anything.[2] Knowing that He cares fills me with a peace that surpasses all understanding.[3]

I cast all my cares on God. No one ever cared for me like Him,[4] and no one cares for me like Him. He knows all about me,[5] and He still loves me.[6] He knows exactly what I need,[7] and He provides it for me.[8] Like a mother cares for her children and a hen cares for her chicks, my Father cares for me.[9]

God takes good care of His property. Therefore, I surrender all I have and am to Him. I trust Him implicitly.[10]

Why should I worry? Why should I fear? It is my Father's good pleasure to give me His kingdom[11] which consists of power, love, and self-control.[12] I receive His kingdom-power in my life right now.[13]

The Lord cares about everyone who trusts in Him.[14] In their behalf, He undertakes to shepherd,[15] guide,[16] heal,[17] bless,[18] and deliver.[19] How I praise Him for His shepherding, guidance, healing, blessing, and deliverance[20] in my life.

The Lord is my Shepherd. I shall never be in want. He makes me lie down in green pastures. He leads me beside quiet waters. He restores my soul. He guides me in the paths of righteousness for His name's sake. Even though I walk through the valley of the shadow of death, I will fear no evil because He walks with me. His rod and staff bring comfort to my soul. He prepares a table before me in the presence of my enemies. He anoints my head with oil. My cup overflows. Surely goodness and mercy and love will follow me all the days of my life, and I will dwell in the Lord's house forever.[21]

References: (1) 1 Peter 5:7; (2) Luke 12:32; (3) Philippians 4:7; (4) 1 Peter 5:7; (5) Psalms 139:1-5; (6) Romans 5:8; (7) Matthew 6:8; (8) Philippians 4:19; (9) Matthew 23:37; (10) Proverbs 3:5-6; (11) Luke 12:32; (12) 2 Timothy 1:7; (13) Acts 1:8; (14) Psalms 145:20; (15) John 10:14; (16) Psalms 32:8; (17) Matthew 4:23; (18) Deuteronomy 15:6; (19) Psalms 37:40; (20) Isaiah 36:15; (21) Psalms 23.

Bible Prayer: Lord God,[1] thank you for caring about me and for me so much.[2] You know the number of hairs on my head,[3] and you are intimately acquainted with all the needs of my life.[4] I feel your care, Father, and I know you understand.[5] I rejoice[6] when I realize that you are touched with the feelings of my infirmities.[7] Truly, your love covers me like a warm and cozy blanket.[8] I will wear that rich and beautiful blanket throughout this day. In Jesus' name,[9] Amen.

References: (1) Psalms 3:3; (2) Psalms 36:7;
(3) Matthew 10:30; (4) Matthew 6:8; (5) Psalms 139:2;
(6) Philippians 3:1; (7) Hebrews 4:15; (8) Isaiah 51:16;
(9) John 16:23.

Related Scriptures: Psalms 8:4; Psalms 55:22; Psalms 65:9; Psalms 144:3; Nahum 1:7; 1 Thessalonians 2:7.

11

GOD IS CHANGING ME

Bible Promise: "Now the Lord is that Spirit: and where the Spirit of the Lord is, there is liberty. But we all, with open face beholding as in a glass the glory of the Lord, are changed into the same image from glory to glory, even as by the Spirit of the Lord" (2 Cor. 3:17-18).

Bible Meditation: I have been born again through the incorruptible seed of the Word of God[1] and by the power of the Holy Spirit.[2] I am a new creation in Christ.[3] The Lord is changing me into the image He desires.[4] It is God who works in me both to will and to do according to His good pleasure.[5] I am His workmanship, created in Christ Jesus unto good works which God ordained me to walk in.[6] He is building my life upon the foundation of the apostles and prophets, with Jesus Christ, my Lord and Savior, as the chief cornerstone. In Him all the building is fitly framed together. Joined with my fellow-believers we are growing into a holy temple in the Lord that we [God's Church] may be a dwelling place in which God lives by His Spirit.[7]

Christ dwells in my heart by faith, and this roots and grounds me in love so that I will be able to comprehend with all saints the breadth and length and depth and height of the love of Christ which passes knowledge, and so I will be filled with all the fullness of God.[8] He is strengthening me with might by His Spirit in my inner person.[9]

God is perfecting me so that I will be able to do the work of the ministry for the edifying of the Body of Christ.[10] His goal for me is that I might arrive at the unity of the faith with my fellow-believers and that I would have understanding and knowledge of God. He wants me to be complete, walking in the measure of the stature of the fullness of Christ.[11] Yes, He is changing me so that I will not be childish any longer. I will no longer be tossed to and fro by every wind of doctrine or by the sleight and craftiness of others.[12] Speaking the truth in love, I will grow up into Christ in all things because He is my Head; He is my Lord.[13]

All things work together for good in my life.[14] God knew me from the foundation of the world.[15] He chose me to become holy and without blame before Him in love.[16] This is His goal for me, and He is changing me into the image of His Son, Jesus Christ.[17] He called me, justified me, and glorified me.[18] God is for me; therefore, who can be against me.[19]

I have put on the new man which is renewed in knowledge after the image of God.[20] God created me in His image.[21] He wants me to take my rightful authority and dominion in every area of my life.[22] When that which is perfect comes, that which is in part will be gone. When I was a child, I spoke like a child, I understood like a child, I thought like a child, but now that God is changing me into a mature believer, I have put all those childish things away. One day I will see my Lord and Savior face to face, and then I shall know even as I am known. Now abide faith, hope, and love, and the greatest of these is love.[23] Because of His great love for me, God is changing me from glory to glory by His Spirit.[4]

References: *(1) 1 Peter 1:23; (2) John 3:6; (3) 2 Corinthians 5:17; (4) 2 Corinthians 3:18; (5) Philippians 2:13; (6) Ephesians 2:10; (7) Ephesians 2:20-22; (8) Ephesians 3:17-19; (9) Ephesians 3:16; (10) Ephesians 4:12; (11) Ephesians 4:13; (12) Ephesians 4:14; (13) Ephesians 4:15; (14) Romans 8:28; (15) Ephesians 1:4; (16) Ephesians 1:4; (17) Romans 8:29; (18) Romans 8:30; (19) Romans 8:31; (20) Colossians 3:10; (21) Genesis 1:27; (22) Genesis 1:28; (23) 1 Corinthians 13:11-13.*

Bible Prayer: Father in heaven,[1] I thank you that you are the Potter in my life.[2] You are molding and shaping me like clay in your hands. Continue your workmanship in my life so that I, as the work of your hands,[3] will be a vessel you can use.[4] I want to be a vessel of honor, sanctified and useful for every good work.[5]

I thank you that you will continue your craftsmanship in my life.[6] The exceeding greatness of your power is at work in my life, Lord,[7] and I believe that you are changing me from glory to glory.[8] You are shaping me according to your eternal purpose in Christ Jesus, my Lord.[9]

In Him I have bold and confident access to you, through faith.[10] For these reasons I bow my knees before you, Father;[11] you are strengthening me with all might by your Spirit deep within me.[12] Christ dwells in my heart by faith so that I will be rooted and grounded in love.[13] You want me to comprehend with all saints the full measure of your love, Father, and you want me to be filled with all your fullness.[14] You are able to do exceeding abundantly above all that I am able to ask or think, according to the power that works within me.[15] Unto you be glory in the Church by Christ Jesus throughout all ages.[16] In Jesus' name I pray,[17] Amen.

References: (1) Jeremiah 3:4; (2) Isaiah 64:8; (3) Isaiah 64:8; (4) Romans 9:21; (5) 2 Timothy 2:21;

(6) Ephesians 2:10; (7) Ephesians 1:19; (8) 2 Corinthians 3:18; (9) Ephesians 3:11; (10) Ephesians 3:12; (11) Ephesians 3:14; (12) Ephesians 3:16; (13) Ephesians 3:17; (14) Ephesians 3:19; (15) Ephesians 3:20; (16) Ephesians 3:21; (17) John 16:24.

Related Scriptures: *1 Corinthians 12:6; 1 Corinthians 12:11; 2 Corinthians 7:10; Ephesians 1:11; Philippians 2:13; Colossians 1:29.*

12

MY FAITH IS GROWING

Bible Promise: "So then faith comes by hearing, and hearing by the Word of God" (Rom. 10:17, NKJV).

Bible Meditation: The Word of God renews my mind so that I may prove what is the good, acceptable, and perfect will of my Father,[1] and it increases my faith.[2] I will wash in the cleansing, sanctifying waters of the Word every day.[3] I am sanctified by the truth of God's holy Word.[4]

His Word accomplishes its intended work in me because it is quick and powerful and sharper than any two-edged sword.[5] God is changing me from glory to glory by the Spirit of the Lord.[6] As I meditate on God's Word my faith grows. As I delight in God's Word I am blessed.[7] I know it is impossible to please God without faith, for anyone who comes to God must believe that He is, and that He is a rewarder of all those who diligently seek Him.[8] Faith is the substance of things hoped for, the evidence of things not seen.[9] Through faith I am able to understand so many things, including that the worlds were framed by the Word of God. This helps me to understand that things which are seen were not made of things which I see. They were made by the unseen hand of God.[10] Therefore, I will walk by faith and not by sight.[11]

Through faith God enables me to subdue kingdoms, work the works of righteousness, obtain all of His promises, and even stop the mouths of lions.[12] Through faith I shall be able to quench the violence of fire, escape the edge of the sword, turn my weakness into strength, become valiant in all struggles, and turn my enemies away.[13] There is great power available through faith in God and His unchanging Word.

I will look unto Jesus who is the Author and Finisher of my faith. He endured the cross for me, and now He is sitting next to God the Father in heaven.[14] He is praying for me even now.[15] Through Him, I realize that the trial of my faith is much more precious than of gold that perishes. As my faith is tried and proved genuine it will result in praise and honor and glory at the appearing of Jesus Christ, my Lord and Savior.[16] Even though I have never physically seen Jesus, I love Him, and it is faith that enables me to do so.[17] Believing fully in Him, I rejoice with a joy that is truly unspeakable and full of glory.[18] This enables me to receive the promise that faith gives, even the salvation of my soul.[19]

Jesus helps me to grow stronger in faith because He promises me that if I will believe, all things will be possible for me.[20] Things will happen in my life in direct proportion to my faith.[21] Faith is the victory that overcomes the world.[22] The prayer of faith will save the sick, and the Lord will raise him up.[23]

The righteousness of God is revealed from faith to faith. This is the process that is taking place in my life. It justifies me before the Father in heaven. I will live by faith.[24] I choose to walk by faith[25] and thereby imitate those who through faith and patience inherit the promises that God has given to me in His Word.[26]

References: *(1) Romans 12:2; (2) Romans 10:17; (3) Ephesians 5:26; (4) John 17:17; (5) Hebrews 4:12; (6) 2 Corinthians 3:18; (7) Psalms 1; (8) Hebrews 11:6; (9) Hebrews 11:1; (10) Hebrews 11:3; (11) 2 Corinthians 5:7; (12) Hebrews 11:33; (13) Hebrews 11:34; (14) Hebrews 12:2; (15) Hebrews 7:25; (16) 1 Peter 1:7; (17) 1 Peter 1:8; (18) 1 Peter 1:8; (19) 1 Peter 1:9; (20) Mark 9:23; (21) Matthew 9:29; (22) 1 John 5:4; (23) James 5:15; (24) Romans 1:17; (25) 2 Corinthians 5:7; (26) Hebrews 6:12.*

Bible Prayer: Heavenly Father,[1] I thank you for your command to have faith in you.[2] I know that this faith comes from hearing, and hearing by the Word of God.[3] For this reason

I will meditate upon your Word day and night.[4]
This will cause me to grow, prosper, and flourish.[5]
It will make me fruitful unto every good work.[6]

I claim the promises of your Word by faith, Father.[7] Your Son, my Lord and Savior, Jesus Christ, has assured me that whatever things I desire, to believe that I receive them from you when I pray, and I shall have them.[8] Therefore, I ask you, Father, to take care of the following situations:_____
_____.

By faith I believe that I now receive your answer to these requests.[9] Thank you, Father, for hastening to perform your Word in my life.[10] In Jesus' name I pray,[11] Amen.

References: (1) Ephesians 1:2; (2) Mark 11:22; (3) Romans 10:17; (4) Psalms 1:2; (5) Psalms 1:3; (6) 2 Timothy 3:17; (7) Hebrews 11:33; (8) Mark 11:24; (9) Mark 11:24; (10) Jeremiah 1:12; (11) John 15:16.

Related Scriptures: Habakkuk 2:4; Matthew 9:22; Matthew 9:29; Matthew 17:20; Luke 7:9; 1 Corinthians 16:13.

13

GOD IS FAITHFUL

Bible Promise: "Your mercy, O Lord, is in the heavens, and Your faithfulness reaches to the clouds" (Ps. 36:5, NKJV).

Bible Meditation: My Father is faithful to me.[1] He has called me into fellowship with His Son, my Lord and Savior, Jesus Christ.[2] Not one word of all His good promises has ever failed.[3] He will never leave me nor forsake me.[4] He will be with me until the end of the age.[5] He is a very present help in my time of need.[6]

Throughout my life I have never seen the righteous forsaken nor his seed begging bread.[7] Even if I lack faith, God remains faithful to me.[8] The Lord knows those who are His.[9] He hears my cry.[10] He knows me by name.[11] He recognizes my voice.[12] I am His servant and He always deals well with me.[13] He is always faithful to His Word.[14] His Word will not return to Him empty, but it will accomplish what He desires and achieve the purpose for which He sent it.[15]

God has promised to faithfully accomplish His promises in my life.[16] He will keep me.[17] His Word never fails.[18] I have experienced His great faithfulness in my heart and in my soul.[19]

God loves me.[20] He is my faithful God who always keeps His covenant with me.[21] The rainbow in the clouds after a storm proves His faithfulness to me.[22]

My great and glorious Father will not permit my foot to be moved. He does not sleep nor slumber. He is always watching over me.[23] My Lord is always there for me.[24] His mercy endures forever.[25]

References: (1) 1 Corinthians 1:9; (2) 1 Corinthians 1:9; (3) 1 Kings 8:56; (4) Hebrews 13:5; (5) Matthew 28:20; (6) Psalms 46:1; (7) Psalms 37:25; (8) 2 Timothy 2:13; (9) 2 Timothy 2:19; (10) Psalms 28:1; (11) Psalms 1:6; (12) Psalms 141:1; (13) Psalms 119:65; (14) Psalms 119:65; (15) Isaiah 55:11; (16) 1 Thessalonians 5:24; (17) Genesis 28:15; (18) Joshua 23:14; (19) Joshua 23:14; (20) 1 John 4:19; (21) Deuteronomy 7:8-9; (22) Genesis 9:16; (23) Psalms 121:3-4; (24) Psalms 46:1; (25) Psalms 136:1.

Bible Prayer: Heavenly Father, I thank you for your great faithfulness.[1] Your faithfulness reaches to the skies,[2] and it even reaches me.[3] Your mercy, O Lord, is in the heavens,[4] and your righteousness is like a great mountain.[5] In your faithfulness you preserve both man and beast.[6] How excellent is your lovingkindness, Father.[7] Because of your love, I am able to put my trust under your wings.[8] I know you will satisfy me abundantly.[9] I shall always be able to drink from the river of your pleasures.[10] Thank you for all you have done, are doing, and always will do in my life. In Jesus' name[11] I pray, Amen.

References: (1) Lamentations 3:23; (2) Psalms 36:5; (3) 1 Corinthians 1:9; (4) Psalms 36:5; (5) Psalms 36:6; (6) Psalms 36:6; (7) Psalms 36:7; (8) Psalms 36:7; (9) Psalms 36:8; (10) Psalms 36:8; (11) John 15:16.

Related Scriptures: Deuteronomy 7:9; Psalms 119:86; Isaiah 49:7; 1 Corinthians 10:13; 2 Thessalonians 3:3.

14

I HAVE NOTHING TO FEAR

Bible Promise: "For God hath not given us the spirit of fear; but of power, and of love, and of a sound mind" (2 Tim. 1:7).

Bible Meditation: My Father in heaven loves me, and it is His good pleasure to give me His kingdom. Therefore, I have no reason whatever to fear.[1] Because I dwell in the secret place of the most high God I shall always abide under the shadow of the Almighty.[2] Nothing shall ever be able to separate me from the love of God which is in Christ Jesus, my Lord.[3] The Lord is my light and my salvation. Because this is true, I have nothing to fear.[4] He is the strength of my life. Of whom, then, should I be afraid?[5] When the wicked, even my enemies, come against me they shall not prevail.[6] Even if a host of foes should encamp against me I will not fear because my confidence is in the Lord.[7]

One thing have I desired of the Lord, and this is what I will continue to seek after — that I may dwell in the house of the Lord all the days of my life, to behold the beauty of the Lord, and to inquire in His temple.[8] In the time of trouble He shall hide me in His pavilion — in the secret of His tabernacle, high upon a rock, and my head will be lifted high above my enemies. This confidence gives me great joy, and I will sing praises unto the Lord.[9]

The Lord is my refuge and my fortress. He is my God, and in Him I will trust.[10] I will trust in Him with all my heart, leaning not unto my own understanding. In all my ways I will acknowledge Him, and I know He will direct my paths.[11] When I call upon Him in a time of stress and difficulty He hears me. He is on my side; therefore, I will not fear.[12] As I let God arise from deep within me, He will scatter all my enemies.[13] No weapon formed against me shall prosper.[14] If God is for me, who can be against me?[15] All things work together for good to me because I love the Lord.[16] I am more than a conqueror through Christ.[17]

There is no fear in love. God's perfect love casts all fear away from me. For this reason, therefore, there is nothing — nothing at all — to fear.[18] I love the Lord because He first loved me.[19]

References: (1) Luke 12:32; (2) Psalms 91:1; (3) Romans 8:38-39; (4) Psalms 27:1; (5) Psalms 27:1; (6) Psalms 27:2; (7) Psalms 27:3; (8) Psalms 27:4; (9) Psalms 27:5-6; (10) Psalms 91:2; (11) Proverbs 3:5-6; (12) Psalms 118:5-6; (13) Psalms 68:1;

(14) Isaiah 54:17; (15) Romans 8:31; (16) Romans 8:28; (17) Romans 8:37; (18) 1 John 4:18; (19) 1 John 4:19.

Bible Prayer: God, my Father,[1] you are my refuge and my strength. You are a very present help in time of trouble.[2] Therefore, I will not fear even if the earth is removed and the mountains are carried into the sea.[3] There is a river which has streams that make the city of God glad.[4] I want to flow in that river, Father. Thank you for being in the midst of your people, Lord. I shall not be moved. You will help me speedily.[5] I will be still and know you as my God. You will be exalted in the earth.[6] Thank you for always being with me.[7] I thank you that no evil will ever befall me, and no plague will come near me or my family. You have given your angels charge over me in order to keep me in all your ways.[8] I will fear no evil because I know you are with me. Your rod and your staff bring me comfort, and I know that goodness and mercy will follow me all the days of my life, and I will dwell in your house forever.[9] In Jesus' name I pray,[10] Amen.

References: (1) 2 John 3; (2) Psalms 46:1; (3) Psalms 46:2; (4) Psalms 46:4; (5) Psalms 46:5; (6) Psalms 46:10; (7) Psalms 46:11; (8) Psalms 91:10-11; (9) Psalms 23:4-6; (10) John 16:24.

Related Scriptures: Luke 2:10; Luke 8:50; Romans 8:15; Hebrews 2:15.

15

CHRISTIAN FELLOWSHIP STRENGTHENS ME

Bible Promise: "But if we walk in the light as He is in the light, we have fellowship with one another, and the blood of Jesus Christ His Son cleanses us from all sin" (1 John 1:7, NKJV).

Bible Meditation: Jesus prayed that I would be one with fellow-believers as He and the Father are one. I believe His Word, and I will do all that is possible to be one with my brothers and sisters in Christ. When the world sees this unity they will believe in my Father in heaven. Jesus has given me all I need to be one with other Christians.[1] His Spirit builds us together upon the foundation of the apostles and prophets — a foundation that has Jesus Christ as its chief cornerstone. With my fellow-believers I am permanently joined — a building that is fitly framed together into a holy temple in the Lord, the habitation of God.[2]

The Lord commands His blessing where the brethren dwell together in unity.[3] I am a member of the Body of Christ, and so are all my brothers and sisters in Him.[4] I will do my part to ensure that there will be no schism in the Lord's body by caring for my fellow-believers.[5]

I will preserve the unity of the Spirit in the bond of peace.[6] I will not forsake the assembling of believers as the manner of some is.[7] I will bear the burdens of my brothers and sisters in Christ, and so fulfill the Law of Christ.[8] When I see a fellow-believer overtaken in a fault, I will make every effort to restore him/her in the spirit of meekness, considering myself lest I should also be tempted in that area.[9] The bond that ties our hearts together is love, and I will make every effort to live in the more-excellent way of love in all my relationships with members of the Body of Christ.[10]

At all times I will be a follower of God in child-like trust.[11] I will walk in love as Christ has loved me. He loved me so much, in fact, that He gave himself as an offering and sacrifice to God in my behalf.[12] I will treat my brothers and sisters with mercy, kindness, meekness, patience, and love — the bond of perfection.[13] I will let the peace of God rule in my heart, and I will be thankful for it as I relate to my fellow-Christians.[14] I will let the Word of Christ dwell in me richly, in all its wisdom, and this will enable me to teach and admonish others in psalms and hymns and spiritual songs as I sing with grace in my heart to the Lord.[15] Whatever I do in word or deed will be done in the name of my Lord and Savior, Jesus Christ. I will always give thanks to God, my Father, through Him.[16]

It is my desire to be like-minded with my brothers and sisters in Christ, sharing His love with them, in one accord and one mind.[17] I will not permit myself to do anything out of strife or pride, but in lowliness of mind I will esteem other believers as better than myself.[18] Through the washing in the water of God's Word,[19] I will renew my mind.[20] I want the mind of Christ to be in control of all my thoughts.[21] The strengthening that comes from Christian fellowship makes my heart rejoice. I will rejoice evermore.[22]

References: (1) John 17:20-23; (2) Ephesians 2:19-22; (3) Psalms 133; (4) 1 Corinthians 12:18; (5) 1 Corinthians 12:25; (6) Ephesians 4:3; (7) Hebrews 10:25; (8) Galatians 6:2; (9) Galatians 6:1; (10) 1 Corinthians 12:31; (11) Ephesians 5:1; (12) Ephesians 5:2; (13) Colossians 3:12-14; (14) Colossians 3:15; (15) Colossians 3:16; (16) Colossians 3:17; (17) Philippians 2:2; (18) Philippians 2:3; (19) Ephesians 5:26; (20) Romans 12:2; (21) Philippians 2:5; (22) 1 Thessalonians 5:16.

Bible Prayer: Lord God,[1] thank you for calling me out of the world and into your Church — the universal fellowship of believers.[2] Help me to remember at all times my obligation to be of like mind with my brothers and sisters, to practice compassion toward them, to love them as family members, and to be courteous to them. You have called me to minister to them, and as I do so, I know I will inherit a blessing from you.[3]

I thank you for the power that exists in the prayer of agreement. If two believers shall agree as touching any thing in heaven or on earth you will do it for them, for where two or three are gathered together in your name, you promise to be there with us.[4] Thank you, Father.

Through the power of your Spirit,[5] I will walk in love toward my brothers and sisters in Christ.[6] I will walk in the light.[7] I will walk in forgiveness.[8] By loving my brothers and sisters I show that I am abiding in the light, and such abiding keeps me from ever stumbling.[9] Father, I thank you for your great faithfulness. You have called me into the fellowship of your Son, my Lord and Savior, Jesus Christ. It is He who enables the members of His body to speak the same thing, be undivided and perfectly joined together in the same mind and judgment.[10]

Lord, I know you want me to do my part, and I know you will enable me to do so, for I am a laborer for and together with you. I am a part of your husbandry, your building.[11] Thank you for making me the temple of your Holy Spirit who lives within me.[12] I am your dwelling-place.[13] Thank you for the sustaining and strengthening power of Christian fellowship in my life. In Jesus' name I pray, Amen.[14]

References: (1) Leviticus 20:24; (2) 1 Corinthians 12:18; (3) 1 Peter 3:8-9; (4) Matthew 18:19-20; (5) Galatians 5:22; (6) Ephesians 5:2; (7) 1 John 1:7; (8) Matthew 18:21-22; (9) 1 John 2:10; (10) 1 Corinthians 1:9-10; (11) 1 Corinthians 3:9; (12) 1 Corinthians 6:19; (13) Ephesians 3:17; (14) John 15:16.

Related Scriptures: Acts 2:42; 1 Corinthians 1:9; 2 Corinthians 6:14; Philippians 2:1; Psalms 133:1-3.

16

FORGIVING OTHERS RELEASES ME

Bible Promise: "For if you forgive men their trespasses, your heavenly Father will also forgive you. But if you do not forgive men their trespasses, neither will your Father forgive your trespasses" (Matt. 6:14-15, NKJV).

Bible Meditation: Forgetting those things which are behind me, and reaching forth unto those things which are ahead, I press toward the mark for the prize of the high calling of God in Christ Jesus.[1] I will be careful to make certain that no root of bitterness springs up in my life, defiling myself and others.[2] I will bear with others and forgive others in the same way Christ Jesus, my Lord, has forgiven me.[3]

The Lord enables me to forget the past, as He brings forth His new thing in my life. He always makes a way for me in the wilderness, and rivers in the desert.[4] Vengeance belongs to Him, and He will recompense the wrongs that are done unto me.[5] I do not have to defend myself because He is my defense.[6]

With all this in mind, I will not let evil overcome me, but I will overcome evil with

good.[7] Instead of rendering evil for evil, I will
bless those who do me wrong. God called me
to respond in this way so that I could inherit a
blessing from Him.[8] He enables me to be
happy when I am persecuted for righteousness'
sake, because I know the Kingdom of Heaven
is mine.[9] When others revile me, persecute me,
and say all manner of evil against me falsely
for the sake of the Lord, I can still be happy.[10]
When these things happen to me, I will rejoice
and be exceeding glad because I know my
reward in heaven will be great.[11]

It brings me joy to realize that I can be a
partaker in the sufferings of Christ,[12] and I
know that the sufferings of this present time are
not to be compared with the glory He is going
to reveal to me.[13] When His glory is revealed, I
will be glad with exceeding joy.[14] I choose to
forgive others freely,[15] no matter how many
times they sin against me.[16]

A forgiving spirit, I realize, is a prerequisite
to power in prayer.[17] As I forgive others, my
Father in heaven forgives me.[18] Forgiving
others releases me.[19] When I am reproached
for the name of Christ I can be happy because I
know the spirit of glory and of God rest upon
me.[20] Therefore, I will put away all bitterness,
wrath, anger, and evil speaking from my life. I
will replace those forms of malice with kindness,

tenderheartedness and forgiveness, even as God for Christ's sake has forgiven me.[21]

References: (1) Philippians 3:13-14; (2) Hebrews 12:15; (3) Colossians 3:13; (4) Isaiah 43:18-19; (5) Hebrews 10:30; (6) Psalms 91:2; (7) Romans 12:21; (8) 1 Peter 3:9; (9) Matthew 5:10; (10) Matthew 5:11; (11) Matthew 5:12; (12) 1 Peter 4:13; (13) Romans 8:18; (14) 1 Peter 4:13; (15) Mark 11:25; (16) Matthew 18:21-22; (17) Mark 11:25; (18) Matthew 6:14; (19) Luke 6:37; (20) 1 Peter 4:14; (21) Ephesians 4:31-32.

Bible Prayer: Lord,[1] your Word is precious to me.[2] I will walk in the light it provides.[3] Through your grace I now choose to forgive the following individuals who have wronged me:

_____

_____. Thank you, Father, for enabling me to walk in your forgiveness and love.[4]

Through your grace I will love my enemies, bless those who curse me, do good to those who hate me, and pray for those who despitefully use me and persecute me.[5] I will not judge others because I know that I will receive the same judgment I give out.[6] Instead of looking at the faults of others, I will examine my own life, and realizing how much I need forgiveness every day, I will mind my own business.[7]

Thank you for forgiving me, Lord,[8] and for calling me to follow in the footsteps of Jesus who did no sin and was completely guileless in every respect.[9] With your help I will be like Him who never reviled when He was reviled, did not threaten others when He suffered, but simply committed everything to you, His Father in heaven.[10] In His name I pray,[11] Amen.

References: (1) Psalms 110:1; (2) 1 Samuel 3:1; (3) Psalms 119:105; (4) Mark 11:25; (5) Matthew 5:44; (6) Matthew 7:1; (7) 1 Thessalonians 4:11; (8) Psalms 103:12; (9) 1 Peter 2:21-22; (10) 1 Peter 2:23; (11) John 16:24.

Related Scriptures: Matthew 6:12; Matthew 9:6; Matthew 18:21; Matthew 18:35; Mark 2:7; Mark 2:10; Luke 23:34; 2 Corinthians 2:10; 1 John 1:9.

17

JESUS HAS SET ME FREE

Bible Promise: "And you shall know the truth, and the truth shall make you free" (John 8:32, NKJV).

Bible Meditation: I know Jesus Christ who is the way, the truth, and the life.[1] He has set me free from the law of sin and death.[2] Because I know the truth of His Word, I am able to walk in freedom.[3] His Word is the Word of truth.[4] There is, therefore, now no condemnation in my life because I am in Christ Jesus, and I walk after the Spirit, not after the flesh.[5]

I'm free from the guilt of the past.[6] I have been justified by faith.[7] I'm free from the fear of the future because God's perfect love casts out all fear.[8] God commended His love toward me, in that while I was yet a sinner, Christ died for me.[9] Now I am truly free, and there is no condemnation in my life whatsoever.[10]

The Father has called me to liberty. I will walk in spiritual liberty and never permit my freedom to be used as an opportunity to serve my flesh. Rather, I will let the liberty I enjoy to freely motivate me to love and serve other people.[11] I will keep on looking into the perfect law of liberty (God's Word). I will not forget the

Lord's teachings. I will walk in His Word, and I know I will be blessed.[12]

Freely I have received. Therefore, I will give freely as well.[13] The Lord, who is the bright and morning star,[14] has invited me to drink freely of the water of life.[15] He has called me to be the salt of the earth,[16] and I will walk in spiritual freedom so that my life will make others thirsty for the water of life.[17] I will invite others to taste and see that the Lord is good,[18] because He has satisfied my spiritual hunger[19] and thirst.[20] Jesus is the Bread of life,[21] and His Word is my daily bread.[22]

The Spirit of the Lord is a Spirit of liberty, and He imparts liberty to me. Wherever He is, there is liberty.[23] I will stand fast, therefore, in the liberty that He has provided for me, and through God's grace I will never again become entangled with the yoke of bondage that used to hold me back.[24]

References: *(1) John 14:6; (2) Romans 8:2; (3) John 8:32; (4) John 17:17; (5) Romans 8:1; (6) Romans 3:24; (7) Romans 5:1; (8) 1 John 4:18; (9) Romans 5:8; (10) Romans 8:1; (11) Galatians 5:13; (12) James 1:25; (13) Matthew 10:8; (14) Revelation 22:16; (15) Revelation 22:17; (16) Matthew 5:13; (17) Revelation 21:6; (18) Psalms 34:8; (19) John 6:35; (20) John 4:13; (21) John 6:35; (22) Matthew 4:4; (23) 2 Corinthians 3:17; (24) Galatians 5:1.*

Bible Prayer: Dear Lord,[1] thank you for saving me from my sin.[2] I believe in your Son, my Lord and Savior, Jesus Christ, who willingly became a propitiation (sacrifice) for my sins.[3] He is the Lamb of God that takes sin away.[4] Thank you for justifying me freely by your grace through the redemption that Jesus Christ provided for me.[5] This is what enables me to enter into the glorious liberty of the sons of God.[6] I am truly free, and I will not use my liberty as a cloak of evil conduct, but as your servant, Father.[7] Thank you for the gift of spiritual freedom. I will walk in freedom because I am truly free.[8] In Jesus' name I pray,[9] Amen.

References: *(1) Malachi 2:16; (2) Romans 6:23; (3) Romans 3:25; (4) John 1:29; (5) Romans 3:24; (6) Romans 8:21; (7) 1 Peter 2:16; (8) Galatians 5:1; (9) John 16:24.*

Related Scriptures: *Romans 6:18; Romans 6:22; 1 Corinthians 7:22.*

FRUITFULNESS

18

I AM CHOSEN TO BEAR FRUIT

Bible Promise: "You did not choose Me, but I chose you and appointed you that you should go and bear fruit, and that your fruit should remain, that whatever you ask the Father in My name He may give you" (John 15:16, NKJV).

Bible Meditation: God chose me.[1] He appointed me to bear lasting fruit for Him.[2] Because He has chosen me I know that when I pray in accordance with His will He will give me whatever I ask in the Name of Jesus.[3] Jesus is the vine, and my heavenly Father is the gardener.[4] Through His Word I am clean.[5] I will abide in Him.[6] Without Jesus Christ, my Lord and Savior, I can do nothing,[7] but through Him I can do all things.[8]

I will continue to abide in Jesus.[9] As I abide in Him, and let His words abide in me, I know I will be able to ask whatever I will and it shall be done unto me.[10] What a great and precious prayer promise this is.[11] God has called[12] and chosen me[13] to be His friend.[14] He reveals His heart and mind to me.[15] There is no greater love than that which was demonstrated by Jesus when He laid down His life for me. He loves me.[16]

The Lord has chosen me for His own inheritance.[17] He has chosen me before the foundation of the world so that I would be holy and without blame before Him in love.[18] He has predestined me to be adopted by Jesus Christ according to the good pleasure of His will,[19] to the praise of the glory of His grace in which I have been accepted in the beloved.[20]

In Christ I have redemption through His blood that was shed for me.[21] He has forgiven all my sins according to the riches of His grace.[22] He has abounded toward me in all wisdom and understanding.[23] He has made known unto me the mystery of His will, according to His good pleasure which He has purposed in himself.[24]

In the dispensation of the fullness of time He will gather me together with all those who know Him.[25] All believers will be gathered together in Him.[26] In Christ Jesus, my Lord, I have obtained an inheritance[27] that goes far beyond all that I could ask or think.[28] He is giving me the spirit of wisdom and revelation in the knowledge of Him.[29] The eyes of my understanding are being enlightened so that I will know the hope of His calling, and the riches of His glorious inheritance in the saints.[30] He is revealing to me the exceeding greatness of His power which is toward me as I exercise faith in Him. This power is like the working of His mighty power which He wrought in Christ when He raised Him from the dead and set Him at His own right hand in heavenly places.[31] He has chosen me to receive all these spiritual riches in great abundance.[32]

Scripture References: (1) *John 15:19;* (2) *John 15:16;* (3) *John 15:16;* (4) *John 15:1;* (5) *John 15:3;* (6) *John 15:5;* (7) *John 15:5;* (8) *Philippians 4:13;* (9) *John 15:7;* (10) *John 15:7;* (11) *2 Peter 1:4;* (12) *2 Timothy 1:9;* (13) *John 15:16;* (14) *John 15:14;* (15) *John 15:15;* (16) *John 15:13;* (17) *Psalms 33:12;* (18) *Ephesians 1:4;* (19) *Ephesians 1:5;* (20) *Ephesians 1:6;* (21) *Ephesians 1:7;* (22) *Ephesians 1:7;* (23) *Ephesians 1:8;* (24) *Ephesians 1:9;* (25) *Ephesians 1:10;* (26) *Ephesians 1:10;* (27) *Ephesians 1:11;* (28) *Ephesians 3:20;* (29) *Ephesians 1:17;* (30) *Ephesians 1:18;* (31) *Ephesians 1:19-20;* (32) *2 Peter 1:3.*

Bible Prayer: Almighty God,[1] I thank you for choosing me.[2] I did not choose you, but you chose me.[3] I will bear much lasting fruit for you because you have chosen me to do so.[4] You have chosen me out of the world, Father,[5] and you have given me your Holy Spirit to be my Comforter,[6] Teacher,[7] Empowerer,[8] and Guide.[9] Thank you, Father, for your great love to me.[10]

It gives me great peace to realize that you know me as one of your chosen ones.[11] It is a privilege for me to be your chosen vessel, and I will bear your name before all those with whom I come in contact.[12] I praise you, Lord, for choosing me from the beginning to receive salvation through sanctification of the Spirit and believing the truth.[13] Through your Gospel I was called and chosen as one who would obtain the glory of the Lord Jesus Christ.[14] Therefore, Father, I will stand fast on your solid Word.[15] Thank you for loving me and giving me everlasting consolation and good hope through grace.[16] My heart is greatly comforted, Lord, as I realize that you will establish me in every good word and work.[17] In Jesus' name[18] I pray, Amen.

References: (1) Genesis 28:3; (2) John 15:16; (3) John 15:16; (4) John 15:16; (5) John 15:19; (6) John 15:26; (7) John 14:26; (8) Acts 1:8; (9) Isaiah 58:11; (10) Romans 5:8; (11) John 14:27; (12) Acts 9:15; (13) 2 Thessalonians 2:13; (14) 2 Thessalonians 2:14; (15) 2 Thessalonians 2:15; (16) 2 Thessalonians 2:16; (17) 2 Thessalonians 2:17; (18) John 15:16.

Related Scriptures: Haggai 2:23; Matthew 20:16; Mark 13:20; Acts 22:14; 1 Peter 2:9.

G O D

19

GOD REIGNS

Bible Promise: "Great is the Lord, and greatly to be praised in the city of our God, in the mountain of his holiness. Beautiful for situation, the joy of the whole earth, is mount Zion, on the sides of the north, the city of the great King" (Ps. 48:1-2).

Bible Meditation: The greatness of the Lord is unsearchable.[1] His kingdom is an everlasting kingdom and His dominion endures throughout all generations.[2] In His greatness, His majesty,[3] and His power,[4] He loves me[5] and He knows what I need before I express it to Him.[6] He is my wonderful Lord, the mighty God, the everlasting Father, and the Prince of Peace.[7]

The everlasting God, my Lord, is the Creator of the universe. He does not faint and He is never tired. He is so great that He goes beyond my ability to comprehend Him.[8] He is always ready to hear my cry.[9] He never slumbers nor sleeps.[10] Even though God is my judge, the lawgiver, the king, He has reached down and saved me.[11]

The magnitude of His greatness is stunning.[12] My heavenly Father is the high and lofty one who inhabits eternity. His name is holy. He lives in the high and holy place with all those who are humble and contrite.[13] He gives grace to the humble.[14] He will not despise the contrition (brokenness) of my heart before Him.[15]

The Lord is my dwelling place as He has been for people of all generations. Before the mountains were brought forth and the earth was created, from everlasting to everlasting, He has been the sovereign Ruler of the universe. He is my God. A thousand years in His sight are but as yesterday when it is past, and as a watch in the night.[16]

I see the Lord sitting upon His throne, high and lifted up, and His train fills the Temple.[17] Holy, holy, holy is the Lord of hosts. The whole earth is filled with His glory.[18]

References: (1) Psalms 145:3; (2) Psalms 145:13; (3) 2 Peter 1:16; (4) Exodus 15:6; (5) John 3:16; (6) Matthew 6:8; (7) Isaiah 9:6; (8) Isaiah 40:25-28; (9) Psalms 34:17; (10) Psalms 121:3; (11) Isaiah 33:22; (12) Psalms 145:3; (13) Isaiah 57:15; (14) 1 Peter 5:5; (15) Psalms 51:17; (16) Psalms 90:1-4; (17) Isaiah 6:1; (18) Isaiah 6:3.

Bible Prayer: Almighty God,[1] the heaven is your throne, and the earth is your footstool. Your hands have made all things, and yet you still have regard for me when I maintain a humble and contrite spirit before you and

when I tremble at your Word.[2]　Thank you,
Father.[3]　You reign, O Lord, and I rejoice.[4]　The
heavens declare your righteousness, and in
your creation I behold your glory.[5]　You are
high above all the earth, and you are exalted
far above all gods.[6]　I love you, and I hate evil.
Thank you for preserving my soul and for
delivering me out of the hand of the wicked.[7]　I
rejoice in you, Father, and I will always give
thanks when I remember your holiness.[8]　In
Jesus' name I pray,[9] Amen.

*References:　(1) Genesis 35:11; (2) Isaiah 66:1-2;
(3) Psalms 147:7; (4) Psalms 97:1; (5) Psalms 97:6;
(6) Psalms 97:9; (7) Psalms 97:10; (8) Psalms 97:12;
(9) John 16:23.*

*Related Scriptures:　Exodus 15:7; Deuteronomy
32:3; 1 Chronicles 29:11; Ephesians 1:19.*

20

GODLINESS WITH CONTENTMENT IS GAIN FOR ME

Bible Promise: "Now godliness with contentment is great gain" (1 Tim. 6:6, NKJV).

Bible Meditation: The Lord will keep me contented and in perfect peace if I keep my mind focused on Him and trust Him with all my heart.[1] I will trust in Him forever, because in Him there is everlasting strength.[2] He supplies all my needs according to His riches in glory by Christ Jesus.[3] He provides me with a supernatural peace that surpasses all understanding.[4] He is my righteousness.[5] He who knew no sin became sin so that I could become righteous.[6]

I have no righteousness or godliness of my own,[7] but through Him I have been made righteous.[8] Great is the mystery of godliness,[9] but I will exercise it in my life because I know it brings contentment to me.[10] Godliness in my life is profitable in all things because it gives me promise for the life that now is and for the life that is to come.[11] I will walk in godliness because I know this will lead to a peaceable and honest life.[12]

I will believe God because He is a Rewarder of all those who diligently seek Him.[13] I will trust Him with all my heart.[14] I will seek first His kingdom and His righteousness, and in so doing I know that everything I need will be provided.[15] I will pray because I know God will answer me and He will reveal great and mighty things to me.[16] He will never leave me nor forsake taking care of me. Therefore, I can be content in my present circumstances and be free from the love of money.[17]

Godliness teaches me that the Lord is my helper. Therefore, I will not fear what man can do to me.[18] I can be content because the Lord is a shield for me. He is my glory and the lifter of my head. When I lie down and sleep, and when I awake, the Lord will sustain me.[19] I will be found in Christ, not having my own righteousness or godliness, but that which is imparted to me through faith — the righteousness of God by faith.[20] These are the reasons why godliness with contentment is great gain for me.[21]

References: (1) Isaiah 26:3; (2) Isaiah 26:4; (3) Philippians 4:19; (4) Philippians 4:7; (5) 1 Corinthians 1:30; (6) 2 Corinthians 5:21; (7) Philippians 3;9; (8) Romans 4:11; (9) 1 Timothy 3:16; (10) 1 Timothy 4:7; (11) 1 Timothy 4:8; (12) 1 Timothy 2:2;

(13) Hebrews 11:6; (14) Proverbs 3:5; (15) Matthew 6:33; (16) Jeremiah 33:3; (17) Hebrews 13:5; (18) Hebrews 13:6; (19) Psalms 3:3-6; (20) Philippians 3:9; (21) 1 Timothy 6:6.

Bible Prayer: Heavenly Father,[1] let the words of my mouth, and the meditation of my heart, be acceptable in your sight. You are my strength and my Redeemer.[2] You are my everlasting righteousness.[3] I will walk in godliness so that others will glorify you.[4] I look for the blessed hope, the glorious appearing and return of my Lord and Savior, Jesus Christ, who gave himself for me in order to redeem me from all iniquity and to purify me.[5] You never leave me nor forsake me,[6] and you provide everything I need.[7] These are some of the reasons why the godliness you've imparted to me and your loving care bring me contentment. This is great gain in my life, Lord,[8] and I thank you for it. In Jesus' name I pray,[9] Amen.

References: *(1) John 6:32; (2) Psalms 19:14; (3) Romans 14:17; (4) Titus 2:12; (5) Titus 2:13-14; (6) Hebrews 13:5; (7) Philippians 4:19; (8) 1 Timothy 6:6; (9) John 16:24.*

Related Scriptures: *Matthew 6:31-34; Hebrews 13:5-6; Romans 8:28.*

21

GOD'S GRACE IS SUFFICIENT FOR ME

Bible Promise: "And He said to me, 'My grace is sufficient for you, for My strength is made perfect in weakness'" (2 Cor. 12:9, NKJV).

Bible Meditation: God's grace is sufficient for me.[1] By His grace, through faith, I was saved.[2] His grace (unmerited favor) provides me with the free gift of salvation.[3] Like Noah of old, I have found grace in the eyes of the Lord.[4] My Savior is Jesus Christ — the incarnate Word of God who is full of grace and truth.[5] I have received of His fullness — grace for grace.[6] How thankful I am that I have been justified freely by His grace.[7] His abundant grace in my life provides me with righteousness that enables me to reign in this life with Him.[8]

God is able to make all grace abound toward me so that I will always have all sufficiency in all things and be able to accomplish many good works.[9] Through His grace He has made me accepted in the beloved.[10] He has blessed me with all spiritual blessings in heavenly places in Christ.[11] Through His grace He chose me in Him before the foundation of the world so that I would be holy and blameless before Him in love.[12]

As a result of His grace I have been redeemed through the blood of Jesus Christ.[13] His grace has forgiven me of all my sins.[14] The riches of His grace have supplied all my needs.[15] I feel truly privileged to be a partaker of God's abounding grace.[16]

God is gracious.[17] He is always ready to pardon, full of mercy and grace.[18] My God is gracious, righteous, and merciful to me.[19] When I was brought low, His grace restored me.[20] He has always dealt bountifully with me.[21] He delivered my soul from death, my eyes from tears, and my feet from falling.[22] Because of His grace in my life I will walk before Him in the land of the living.[23] I know that my Father is a gracious God who is always merciful, slow to anger, and of great kindness.[24] Truly His grace is always sufficient for me.

References: *(1) 2 Corinthians 12:9; (2) Ephesians 2:8; (3) Ephesians 2:8; (4) Genesis 6:8; (5) John 1:14; (6) John 1:16; (7) Romans 3:24; (8) Romans 5:17; (9) 2 Corinthians 9:8; (10) Ephesians 1:6; (11) Ephesians 1:3; (12) Ephesians 1:4; (13) Ephesians 1:7; (14) Ephesians 1:7; (15) Philippians 4:19; (16) Ephesians 1:7-8; (17) Exodus 34:6; (18) Nehemiah 9:17; (19) Psalms 116:5; (20) Psalms 116:6; (21) Psalms 116:7; (22) Psalms 116:8; (23) Psalms 116:9; (24) Jonah 4:2.*

Bible Prayer: O Lord, my gracious God,[1] I thank you for your grace which is greater than all my sin.[2] You have bestowed your marvelous grace upon my life.[3] All your promises are for me.[4] I truly abound in your grace[5] which is always sufficient for me.[6] Your Son, my Lord and Savior, Jesus Christ, is gracious like you are, Father.[7] Though He was rich, for my sake He became poor so that through His poverty I might be made rich.[8] This is true grace in my life, Lord. I receive your grace in my life as a gift that I cannot earn, but I simply receive it because I know you love me and have given it to me.[9] In Jesus' name,[10] Amen.

References: (1) Exodus 34:6; (2) Ephesians 2:5; (3) 2 Corinthians 8:1; (4) 2 Corinthians 7:1; (5) 2 Corinthians 8:7; (6) 2 Corinthians 12:9; (7) 2 Thessalonians 3:18; (8) 2 Corinthians 8:9; (9) Romans 6:23; (10) John 15:16.

Related Scriptures: Acts 4:33; Romans 5:2; Romans 5:15; Romans 5:17; Romans 5:20; Romans 5:21; 1 Corinthians 3:10; 1 Corinthians 15:10; James 4:6; 1 Peter 3:7.

22

GOD IS GUIDING ME

Bible Promise: "The Lord will guide you continually, And satisfy your soul in drought, And strengthen your bones; You shall be like a watered garden, And like a spring of water, whose waters do not fail." (Isa. 58:11, NKJV).

Bible Meditation: A mother eagle stirs up her nest. She flutters her wings over her young. She bears them up on her wings, and so does God take care of me and lead me.[1] He guides me with His eye.[2] He feeds me according to the integrity of my heart, and He guides me by the skillfulness of His hands.[3] The Lord goes before me, and the God of Israel is my rear guard.[4]

God guides me in judgment.[5] He guides me in what is right and He teaches me His way.[6] He is good and upright and that is why He teaches me His ways.[7] In the Lord I have taken refuge. He will never let me be ashamed.[8] He is my rock of refuge and He is my fortress.[9] Since He is my rock and my fortress, and for the sake of His name, He will guide me and lead me.[10]

I choose Him to be my guide unto death, for He is my God forever and ever.[11] He guides me with the counsel of His Word.[12] He holds my hand.[13] The Lord will guide me continually, and satisfy my soul in drought. He makes me like a watered garden and like a spring of water that shall never fail.[14] The Lord directs my steps.[15]

He has been my guide since my youth.[16] He guides my feet in the way of peace.[17] His Spirit guides me into all truth.[18] My spirit is the Lord's candle that searches all the inner depths of my heart.[19] I will trust in the Lord with all my heart and not lean to my own understanding. In all my ways I will acknowledge Him, and He will direct my paths.[20]

The Lord is my Shepherd.[21] He is my Good Shepherd.[22] He leads me beside still waters.[23] He restores my soul, and leads me in the paths of righteousness for His name's sake.[24] Surely goodness and mercy will follow me all the days of my life, and I will dwell in the house of the Lord forever.[25]

References: (1) Deuteronomy 32:11-12; (2) Psalms 32:8; (3) Psalms 78:72; (4) Isaiah 52:12; (5) Psalms 25:9; (6) Psalms 25:9; (7) Psalms 25:8; (8) Psalms 31:1; (9) Psalms 31:3; (10) Psalms 31:3; (11) Psalms 48:14; (12) Psalms 73:24; (13) Psalms 73:23; (14) Isaiah 58:11; (15) Proverbs 16:9; (16) Jeremiah 3:4; (17) Luke 1:79;(18)John 16:13; (19) Proverbs 20:27; (20) Proverbs 3:5-6; (21) Psalms 23:1; (22) John 10:11; (23) Psalms 23:2; (24) Psalms 23:3; (25) Psalms 23:6.*

Bible Prayer: Dear Lord,[1] thank you for being my guide.[2] It is an adventure to be led by your Spirit each day of my life.[3] I thank you that you are not slack regarding your promise. You are always patient as you guide me each step of the way.[4] You reveal your secrets to me.[5] You lead me in right paths.[6] I will walk in the Spirit as you lead me, and I know I will not fulfill the lusts of my flesh.[7] I want always to be led by your Spirit, Lord.[8] In Jesus' name I pray,[9] Amen.

References: (1) Malachi 2:2; (2) Psalms 48:14; (3) Romans 8:14; (4) 2 Peter 3:9; (5) Amos 3:7; (6) Proverb 4:11; (7) Galatians 5:16; (8) Galatians 5:18; (9) John 15:16.

Related Scriptures: Psalms 5:8; Psalms 25:5; Psalms 27:11; Proverbs 8:20; Isaiah 57:18.

HAPPINESS

23

JESUS WANTS ME TO BE HAPPY

Bible Promise: "Blessed are you when people insult you, persecute you and falsely say all kinds of evil against you because of me. Rejoice and be glad, because great is your reward in heaven, for in the same way they persecuted the prophets who were before you" (Matt. 5:11-12, NIV).

Bible Meditation: God has blessed me in so many ways.[1] He wants to give me the desires of my heart.[2] To be blessed is to be happy, and spiritually prosperous, enjoying God's favor. I am happy whenever I remember His benefits to me.[3] He blesses me,[4] and I will bless Him.[5] He satisfies my mouth with good things so that my youth is renewed.[6] He has forgiven all my iniquities and He heals all my diseases.[7] He has redeemed my life from destruction, and He has crowned me with His lovingkindness and His tender mercies.[8] Truly, I am blessed and happy in the Lord.

The Lord is merciful and gracious. He is slow to anger and He is plenteous in mercy.[9] He has not dealt with me according to my sins.[10] As the heaven is high above the earth,

so great is His mercy toward me.[11] As far as
the east is from the west, so far has He
removed my transgressions from me.[12] Like a
father who has compassion for his children,
my heavenly Father has compassion on me.[13]
His mercy is from everlasting to everlasting
upon me because I reverence His name and
obey His commandments.[14] In Him I find my
happiness.[15]

Happiness comes from obeying the Lord.[16]
I am happy because I have found the wisdom
of God's Word.[17] I trust in Him and in His
Word, and this gives me great blessing and
happiness.[18] I will walk in the ways of the
Lord and reverence His name, and this will
make me happy.[19] I will always be happy
because God is my Lord.[20]

References: *(1) Psalms 128:5; (2) Psalms 37:4;*
(3) Psalms 103:2; (4) Psalms 103:5; (5) Psalms 103:1;
(6) Psalms 103:5; (7) Psalms 103:3; (8) Psalms 103:4;
(9) Psalms 103:8; (10) Psalms 103:10; (11) Psalms
103:11; (12) Psalms 103:12; (13) Psalms 103:13;
(14) Psalms 103:17-18; (15) James 5:11; (16) John
13:17; (17) Proverbs 3:13; (18) Proverbs 16:4;
(19) Psalms 128:1; (20) Psalms 144:15.

Bible Prayer: Lord God,[1] thank you for giving
me happiness,[2] gladness,[3] a merry heart,[4] joy,[5]
and countless blessings.[6] As I depend totally
upon you I experience the happiness of your

kingdom.[7]   Thank you for the comfort you provide that leads me to happiness.[8] I will walk in meekness because I know this is the key to the happiness that comes from inheriting the earth.[9] As I hunger and thirst for righteousness I know you will fill me, and this certainty makes me happy indeed.[10] I will be merciful because I have received the happiness that your mercy toward me provides.[11] Purify my heart, Lord, so that I will see you;[12] this will fill my heart with happiness. I will be a peacemaker for you, Lord, and I know this will make me happy as your child.[13] Thank you for making me happy and blessed in every way. In Jesus' name I pray,[14] Amen.

References: *(1) Daniel 9:3; (2) Psalms 144:15; (3) Psalms 4:7; (4) Proverbs 17:22; (5) Nehemiah 8:10; (6) Psalms 103:2; (7) Matthew 5:3; (8) Matthew 5:4; (9) Matthew 5:5; (10) Matthew 5:6; (11) Matthew 5:7; (12) Matthew 5:8; (13) Matthew 5:9; (14) John 16:23.*

Related Scriptures: *Psalms 4:7; Psalms 30:11; Psalms 45:7; Psalms 100:2; Luke 1:14; Hebrews 1:9.*

24

HEALING AND HEALTH ARE MINE

Bible Promise: "Bless the Lord, O my soul, And forget not all His benefits: Who forgives all your iniquities, Who heals all your diseases" (Ps. 103:2-3, NKJV).

Bible Meditation: Jesus, my Savior and Lord, is the Great Physician.[1] He went about doing good and healing all who were oppressed by the devil.[2] He was anointed to preach the gospel to the poor, to heal the broken hearted, to preach deliverance to the captives and recovery of sight to the blind, to set at liberty those that are bruised.[3] He is the same yesterday, today, and forever.[4] He forgives all my iniquities and heals all my diseases.[5] He has set me free.[6] He has healed my heart.[7] He has given me freedom.[8] He has loved me with an everlasting love.[9] He is my Lord,[10] my Redeemer,[11] my Savior,[12] my Healer,[13] and He is the One who heals me.[14] He took my infirmities and bore my sicknesses.[15] By His stripes I am healed[16] and I will walk in my healing. I will walk in divine health.

It is so wonderful to know that my Lord wants me to prosper and to be in health.[17] He

sends forth His Word, and heals me.[18] He has
made me whole.[19] I am complete in Him.[20]
He is the One in whom I live, and move, and
have my being.[21] He has risen with healing
in His wings.[22] He has promised good health
to me.[23]

Healing and health come from the Lord.[24]
He loves me and wants me to be healthy. I
claim His promise to make my body healthy
and strong. I will wait upon the Lord and
renew my strength, and I will mount up with
wings as an eagle does.[25] He makes my heart
merry and it does me good like a medicine.[26]
Through His Spirit my body is quickened.[27] I
experience the resurrection-power of Jesus
Christ, my Lord.[28]

My Father anoints me with joy.[29] This is
health to me. The Lord is the Balm in Gilead[30]
who brings healing and health to my body and
soul. I receive His healing and health, and I will
walk in His promise of health throughout this
day.[31] The devil is a liar — the father of lies[32] —
and one of his worst lies is that sickness is God's
will. Through the precious and powerful blood
of Jesus Christ and the word of my testimony,
I will overcome all the attacks that the devil
brings against me.[33] The Bible assures me that
God's will for me is healing and health.[34]

References: *(1) Matthew 15:30; (2) Acts 10:38;
(3) Luke 4:18; (4) Hebrews 13:8; (5) Psalms 103:3;
(6) Galatians 5:1; (7) Psalms 147:3; (8) John 8:36;
(9) Psalms 100:5; (10) 2 Corinthians 1:2; (11) Job
19:25; (12) John 4:42; (13) Isaiah 30:26; (14) Exodus
15:26; (15) Matthew 8:17; (16) Isaiah 53:5;
(17) 3 John 2; (18) Psalms 107:20; (19) John 5:15;
(20) Colossians 2:10; (21) Acts 17:28; (22) Malachi
4:2; (23) 3 John 2; (24) Matthew 9:35; (25) Isaiah
40:31; (26) Proverbs 17:22; (27) Romans 8:11;
(28) Philippians 3:10; (29) Hebrews 1:9;
(30) Jeremiah 8:22; (31) Mark 11:24; (32) John 8:44;
(33) Revelation 12:11; (34) 3 John 2.*

Bible Prayer: Dear Heavenly Father, thank
you that you hasten to perform your Word.[1]
Your Word is quick, and powerful, and sharper
than any two-edged sword.[2] You tell me in
your Word that healing is your children's
bread,[3] that you are the Lord that heals me,[4]
and that Jesus took my infirmities and bore my
sicknesses.[5] I believe your Word that assures me
that whatever things I desire, when I pray, to
believe I receive them from you, Father, and I
shall have them.[6] Therefore, I receive your
healing now, Lord, in my area of physical need
of _____

_____. I believe you are
restoring me to health and vitality. My faith
rests not in the wisdom of men, but in your
great power, O Lord.[7]

With all that is in me, Father, I bless your holy name and I will not forget the benefits of your great mercy. You forgive all my iniquities and you heal all my diseases.[8]

References: (1) Jeremiah 1:12; (2) Hebrews 4:12; (3) Mark 7:27; (4) Exodus 15:26; (5) Matthew 8:17; (6) Mark 11:24; (7) 1 Corinthians 2:5; (8) Psalms 103:3.

Related Scriptures: Matthew 9:35; Isaiah 53:5; John 16:23; Psalms 107:20; Jeremiah 17:14; Matthew 9:22; Mark 1:34; Acts 10:38; 1 Corinthians 12:9; James 4:7.

25

HEAVEN IS MY HOME

Bible Promise: "In My Father's house are many mansions; if it were not so, I would have told you. I go to prepare a place for you. And if I go and prepare a place for you, I will come again and receive you to Myself; that where I am, there you may be also" (John 14:2-3, NKJV).

Bible Meditation: This world is not my home. My citizenship is in heaven. Jesus is preparing a place for me in heaven where I can live with Him forever.[1] Hallelujah! What a Savior! He is the way, the truth, and the life, and He is the only way to my heavenly Father.[2] How it fills me with anticipation to realize that heaven is my true home. Eternal life is mine.[3]

To be absent from the body is to be present with the Lord.[4] God is the Creator of heaven and earth.[5] His holy dwelling place is in heaven, and one day I will dwell there with Him.[6] His kingdom is near.[7] The day is soon to come when Jesus will bring all things in heaven and earth together under His Lordship.[8]

My home in heaven is an eternal house that is not built with human hands.[9] My name is written in heaven in the Lamb's Book of

Life.[10] One day I will join with the saints of all ages in worshiping and praising God.[11]

My Father has given me eternal life through Jesus Christ.[12] His Word is eternal.[13] After my work on this earth is finished, I will go to my eternal home. I take hold of the eternal life He has promised to me.[14]

God has called me to His eternal glory in Christ.[15] He is restoring me and making me strong, firm, and steadfast.[16] I love my Father, and He loves me.[17] I will lay up treasures in heaven[18] while serving as God's ambassador on earth.[19]

References: (1) John 14:1-6; (2) John 14:6; (3) John 3:16; (4) 2 Corinthians 5:8; (5) Genesis 1; (6) Colossians 1:5; (7) Luke 10:9; (8) Colossians 1:20; (9) 2 Corinthians 5:1; (10) Revelation 21:27; (11) Revelation 5:14; (12) Romans 6:23; (13) Psalms 119:89; (14) 1 John 5:13; (15) 1 Peter 2:9; (16) 1 Corinthians 15:58; (17) 1 John 4:19; (18) Matthew 6:20; (19) 2 Corinthians 5:20.

Bible Prayer: My Father in heaven,[1] I praise you and thank you for the promise of eternal life[2] which I now possess through faith in your Son, Jesus Christ, my Lord.[3] It is wonderful to know that He is preparing a place for me in heaven even now.[4] I look forward to the day, Father, when I will be present with you, adoring and worshiping you forever.[5] Thank you for the crown of life that you have reserved for me in heaven.[6] In Jesus' name,[7] Amen.

References: *(1) Matthew 11:25; (2) Ephesians 2:8-9; (3) Romans 10:8-10; (4) John 14:1-6; (5) Revelation 4:11; (6) James 1:12; (7) John 15:16.*

Related Scriptures: *Genesis 1:1; Deuteronomy 33:27; 1 Kings 8:30; Psalms 16:11; Isaiah 66:1; Matthew 3:2; Matthew 5:12; Matthew 6:20; Matthew 28:18; Luke 18:22; 2 Corinthians 5:1; Ephesians 1:10; Philippians 3:20.*

HOLY SPIRIT

26

I AM A TEMPLE OF THE HOLY SPIRIT

Bible Promise: "Do you not know that you are the temple of God and that the Spirit of God dwells in you?" (1 Cor. 3:16, NKJV).

Bible Meditation: The Spirit of God dwells in me.[1] He gives life to my body[2] and He bears witness with my spirit that I am a child of God.[3] The Spirit helps me when I do not always know how to pray effectively, and He makes intercession for me with groanings that cannot be uttered. He makes intercession for me according to the will of God.[4]

My eye has not seen and my ear has not heard all the things the Lord has prepared for me because I love Him.[5] God is revealing these things to me by His Spirit; His Spirit always searches the deep things of God.[6] I have received God's Spirit so that I would be able to know the things that God has freely given to me.[7]

The fruit of the Spirit in my life is love, joy, peace, longsuffering, gentleness, goodness, faith, meekness, temperance, and there is no law against any of these things.[8] The Spirit lives in me,[9] I live in Him,[10] and I will continue to walk in Him.[11] The Spirit of God will lead me.[12] He will teach me all things and bring to my remembrance the things that Jesus taught.[13]

The Holy Spirit gives me joy.[14] He gives me power to witness.[15] He overcomes the enemy in my behalf.[16] He gives me liberty.[17] He changes me from within.[18] He teaches me what to say.[19] He comforts me.[20] He guides me into all truth and tells me things to come.[21] He gives me boldness.[22] He is the Spirit of truth.[23] He fills me with Himself.[24]

References: (1) 1 Corinthians 3:16; (2) Romans 8:11; (3) Romans 8:16; (4) Romans 8:27; (5) 1 Corinthians 2:9; (6) 1 Corinthians 2:10; (7) 1 Corinthians 2:12; (8) Galatians 5:22-23; (9) Romans 8:11; (10) Galatians 5:25; (11) Romans 8:1; (12) Romans 8:14; (13) John 14:26; (14) 1 Thessalonians 1:6; (15) Acts 1:8; (16) Isaiah 59:19; (17) 2 Corinthians 3:17; (18) 2 Corinthians 3:18; (19) Luke 12:12; (20) John 14:16; (21) John 16:13; (22) Acts 4:31; (23) John 14:17; (24) Ephesians 5:18.

Bible Prayer: Heavenly Father,[1] thank you for the Holy Spirit.[2] He reminds me that if I ask anything in the name of Jesus Christ, you will do it for me.[3] I love you, and I want to keep all your commandments.[4] It's so wonderful to realize that Jesus sent the Holy Spirit to be my Comforter, and I know He will abide with me forever.[5]

He is the Spirit of truth, and I am privileged to know Him because He dwells with me and within me.[6] He teaches me all things and brings to my remembrance the things that Jesus has taught.[7] He convicts me of sin.[8] He convinces me of righteousness.[9] He guides me into all truth, and He shows me things to come.[10] He glorifies Jesus Christ.[11] Thank you, Father, for the Holy Spirit.

He assures me that when I ask I shall receive, when I seek I shall find, and when I knock the door shall be opened for me.[12] You have fulfilled your promise in my life by filling me with the Holy Spirit when I asked you to do so.[13] Therefore, I will always thank you, Lord, in the name of Jesus Christ,[14] Amen.

References: (1) Luke 12:30; (2) Romans 15:19; (3) John 14:14; (4) John 14:15; (5) John 14:16; (6) John 14:17; (7) John 14:26; (8) John 16:8; (9) John 16:10; (10) John 16:13; (11) John 16:14; (12) Luke 11:10; (13) Luke 11:13; (14) Ephesians 5:20.

Related Scriptures: Acts 2:17-18; Jude 20-21; 2 Peter 1:20-21.

27

JESUS IS PRAYING FOR ME

Bible Promise: "Therefore He is also able to save to the uttermost those who come to God through Him, since He always lives to make intercession for them" (Heb. 7:25, NKJV).

Bible Meditation: The Lord Jesus Christ is my High Priest.[1] He is praying for me now.[2] He is touched with the feelings of my infirmities.[3] My weakness is His opportunity to prove His strength.[4] Through Him I can do all things.[5] He truly understands me.[6] He knows what I need.[7] My Lord and Savior is the Mediator between me and God, the Father,[8] and He always lives to make intercession in my behalf.[9]

Jesus knows the power of prayer.[10] Through prayer He learned the Father's will.[11] He gained strength to overcome temptation through prayer.[12] He developed a deeply intimate, personal relationship with His Father through prayer.[13] He taught me how to pray,[14] and stressed its importance in my life.[15]

No temptation has come to me but such as is common to all people.[16] My God is able to keep me from all temptation, and to deliver me from the evil one.[17] Jesus and the angels are fighting in my behalf. Jesus has already won the battle.[18] Tempted in all points even as I have been, Jesus never sinned.[19] Now that He lives within me and continues to intercede in my behalf, the power of His Spirit will help me win all my personal battles.[20]

Jesus prayed that God would supply my daily bread,[21] and He always does. He prayed that God's kingdom would come to earth,[22] and now the King resides within me.[23] In fact, the Kingdom of God is within me.[24] That wonderful kingdom is not meat and drink, but it is righteousness, peace, and joy in the Holy Ghost.[25]

Jesus prayed that I and the Father would be one as He and the Father are one,[26] and this has opened the door to a closer relationship with my Father in heaven.[27] Jesus prayed that my sins would be forgiven,[28] and I have been set free.[29] He has redeemed me from the hands of the enemy.[30] His Spirit now prays within me with groanings that cannot be uttered.[31] It is thrilling to realize that the power of the prayers of Jesus undergirds me.

References: *(1) Hebrews 9:11; (2) Hebrews 7:25;*
(3) Hebrews 4:15; (4) 2 Corinthians 12:9;
(5) Philippians 4:13; (6) Psalms 139:23-24;
(7) Matthew 6:8; (8) 1 Timothy 2:5; (9) Hebrews 7:25;
(10) Luke 6:12; (11) Mark 14:36; (12) Luke 22:39-46;
(13) John 17; (14) Luke 11:1-13; (15) Matthew 21:13;

(16) 1 Corinthians 10:13; (17) Luke 11:4; (18) John 19:30; (19) Hebrews 4:15; (20) Ephesians 6:10; (21) Luke 11:3; (22) Luke 11:2; (23) Colossians 1:27; (24) Luke 17:21; (25) Romans 14:17; (26) John 17:21; (27) John 17:23; (28) Luke 11:4; (29) Galatians 5:1; (30) Psalms 107:2; (31) Romans 8:26.

Bible Prayer: Dear Father,[1] I come to you in the full knowledge that Jesus cares.[2] He has made it possible for me to have direct access to you.[3] He has atoned for my sins.[4] The Lord Jesus Christ is the way, the truth, and the life.[5] Because this is true, I am able to approach your throne with confidence,[6] knowing that you hear me and you undertake to answer my prayers.[7] I know that you hear your Son praying for me, and I thank you for answering those prayers. In Jesus' name I pray,[8] Amen.

References: *(1) John 10:15; (2) 1 Peter 5:7; (3) Luke 23:45; (4) Romans 5:11; (5) John 14:6; (6) Hebrews 4:16; (7) 1 John 5:14; (8) John 15:16.*

Related Scriptures: *Psalms 6:9; Psalms 65:2; Matthew 21:22; Acts 10:31; 1 Timothy 4:5; 1 Peter 3:12.*

28

JESUS LIVES!

Bible Promise: "I am He who lives, and was dead, and behold, I am alive forevermore. Amen. And I have the keys of Hades and of Death" (Rev. 1:18, NKJV).

Bible Meditation: Because Jesus lives[1] I have no fear.[2] Because He lives in me[3] I know I can overcome all obstacles in my path.[4] He is the Lord of lords,[5] and the King of kings.[6] I am determined to know Him[7] and the power of His resurrection[8] in my life.

Jesus died for me,[9] and rose again[10] so that I will never have to face a hopeless death,[11] but will instead live with Him forever.[12] My heavenly Father has delivered me from the power of darkness, and translated me into the Kingdom of His dear Son.[13] Through the blood of Jesus Christ I have redemption, even the forgiveness of my sins.[14] Because He lives I know that if I confess my sins, God, who is faithful and just, will forgive me and cleanse me from all unrighteousness.[15] Jesus ever lives to make intercession for me.[16]

My risen Lord created all things in heaven and on earth, both things that are visible and things that are invisible.[17] He is before all things, and by Him all things consist.[18] I want Him to have the preeminence in my life at all times.[19] All fullness dwells in Jesus.[20] My heavenly Father is reconciling all things unto himself through Jesus.[21] In Christ I am made complete.[22] God is making known the riches of His glory to me because the living Christ, my hope of glory, lives within me.[23]

I will let the peace of God rule in my heart.[24] I will let the word of Christ dwell in me richly in all wisdom.[25] Because I know my Savior lives I will do everything in His name, giving thanks to God, my Father.[26] I can do all things through Jesus Christ because He gives me strength.[27] Without Him, I can do nothing.[28] He is the living vine,[29] and I abide in Him.[30]

References: (1) *Revelation 1:18;* (2) *1 John 4:18;* (3) *Colossians 1:27;* (4) *1 John 2:13;* (5) *1 Timothy 6:15;* (6) *Revelation 19:16;* (7) *Philippians 3:8;* (8) *Philippians 3:10;* (9) *Romans 5:8;* (10) *Romans 14:9;* (11) *John 3:16;* (12) *John 4:14;* (13) *Colossians 1:13;* (14) *Colossians 1:14;* (15) *1 John 1:9;* (16) *Hebrews 7:25;* (17) *Colossians 1:16;* (18) *Colossians 1:17;* (19) *Colossians 1:18;* (20) *Colossians 1:19;* (21) *Colossians 1:20;* (22) *Colossians 2:10;* (23) *Colossians 1:27;* (24) *Colossians 3:15;* (25) *Colossians 3:16;* (26) *Colossians 3:17;* (27) *Philippians 4:13;* (28) *John 15:5;* (29) *John 15:1;* (30) *John 15:4.*

Bible Prayer: Lord God,[1] thank you for sending Jesus Christ to be my Lord[2] and Savior.[3] I love Him because He first loved me.[4] How I praise[5] you, Father,[6] that you have given me the victory through Jesus Christ, my Lord.[7] Because He lives, death no longer has a sting and the grave no longer has any victory.[8] Because He lives, I am set free.[9]

Help me, Father, to do the works of Jesus Christ.[10] Thank you for your amazing promise that believers shall be able to do greater works than those Jesus did because He lives with you in heaven.[11] Your Son, my Lord and Savior, Jesus Christ, is in you, Father, and you are in Him.[12] Because this is true, I know that whatever I shall ask in the name of Jesus will be done so that you will be glorified in your Son.[13] I pray these things in Jesus' name,[14] Amen.

References: *(1) Ezekiel 36:2; (2) 1 Timothy 1:1; (3) 2 Peter 2:20; (4) 1 John 4:19; (5) Psalms 119:171; (6) Matthew 16:17; (7) 1 Corinthians 15:57; (8) 1 Corinthians 15:54-56; (9) John 8:32; (10) John 14:12; (11) John 14:12; (12) John 14:10; (13) John 14:13; (14) John 16:23.*

Related Scriptures: *Acts 1:21; Acts 2:31; Acts 4:2; Acts 4:33; Acts 17:18; Acts 17:32; 1 Peter 1:3; 1 Peter 3:21.*

29

JESUS IS COMING SOON!

Bible Promise: "And if I go and prepare a place for you, I will come again and receive you to Myself; that where I am, there you may be also" (John 14:3, NKJV).

Bible Meditation: Jesus is my Lord[1] and Savior.[2] I love Him[3] and He loves me.[4] There is no reason for my heart ever to be troubled because I believe in God and I believe in His Son, Jesus Christ.[5] In my Father's house there are many mansions, and Jesus has gone there to prepare a place for me.[6] One day He will return in order to receive me unto himself so that I will be able to dwell with Him forever.[7] Jesus Christ is the Way, the Truth, and the Life, and no one is able to go to the Father except through Him.[8]

Because I received Him as my personal Savior and believed in His matchless name, He gave me the power to become His child.[9] This assurance of my salvation gives me great peace — a peace that the world cannot give. Therefore, I have no reason to be troubled about anything.[10] I look forward to the day when the trumpet of God shall sound, and the dead in Christ shall be raised. On that great resurrection morning the Lord himself will descend with a shout, and if I am still on the earth at that time, I will be caught up in the clouds to meet the Lord in the air, and so shall I ever be with the Lord.[11] My prayer is that He will come quickly.[12]

References: (1) Jude 4: (2) 2 Peter 1:11; (3) 1 John 4:19; (4) John 3:16; (5) John 14:1; (6) John 14:2; (7) John 14:3; (8) John 14:6; (9) John 1:12; (10) John 14:27; (11) 1 Thessalonians 4:16-17; (12) Revelation 22:20.

Bible Prayer: Come quickly, Lord Jesus.[1] Thank you for loving me so much that you want to return to take me with you.[2] I know you are preparing a marriage banquet for me.[3] Your banner over me is love.[4] Thank you for choosing me.[5] You have chosen me to be a part of your church, your bride.[6] I look forward to the time of your return when you will take me to be with you forever.[7] Thank you, Lord. In Jesus' name I pray,[8] Amen.

References: (1) Revelation 22:20; (2) John 14:3; (3) Revelation 19:7; (4) Song of Solomon 2:4; (5) John 15:16; (6) Revelation 19:7; (7) John 14:3; (8) John 16:24.

Related Scriptures: 1 Corinthians 1:7; 1 Corinthians 15:23; 1 Thessalonians 2:19; 1 Thessalonians 3:13; 1 Thessalonians 4:15; James 5:8.

30

JESUS IS EVERYTHING TO ME

Bible Promise: "Jesus said to him, 'I am the way, the truth, and the life. No one comes to the Father except through Me. If you had known Me, you would have known My Father also; and from now on you know him and have seen Him'" (John 14:6-7, NKJV).

Bible Meditation: Jesus is my Lord[1] and my Savior.[2] Without Him I can do nothing.[3] Through Him, I can do all things because He strengthens me.[4] He is my righteousness.[5] He knew no sin, but even so He became sin for me so that I might become the righteousness of God in Him.[6]

He is the King of kings[7] and the Lord of lords.[8] He is the way, the truth, and the life.[9] He is the one mediator between me and the Father.[10] He is my friend.[11] He sticks closer than any brother.[12] I am a joint-heir with Jesus Christ.[13] I am a co-laborer with Him.[14] He is the Vine; I am a branch of the vine.[15]

He is the door.[16] He is the Good Shepherd,[17] the Great Physician,[18] my Master,[19] and my burden-bearer.[20] He is my example,[21] my High Priest,[22] and my Deliverer.[23] He lives in me.[24]

He is the Light of my life,[25] the Bread of life,[26] the Sun of righteousness,[27] the Rose of Sharon and the lily of the valleys,[28] the bright and morning star,[29] the wonderful counselor,[30] the Prince of peace,[31] the everlasting Father,[32] the mighty God,[33] the Son of God,[34] the son of man,[35] my Redeemer,[36] the captain of my salvation,[37] and the One in whom I live and move and have my being.[38]

Jesus is the Word made flesh.[39] He is Emmanuel — God with us.[40] In Him all the fullness of the Godhead dwells bodily.[41] I am complete in Him.[42] In Him all things hold together.[43] All the treasures of wisdom and knowledge are in Him.[44] Truly, the Lord Jesus Christ is everything to me; He is the Alpha and Omega, the beginning and the end, the first and the last.[45] All authority in heaven and in earth has been given unto Him.[46] God has rightly exalted Him and has given Him a name which is above every name: that at the Name of Jesus every knee should bow, and every tongue confess that Jesus Christ is Lord, to the glory of God the Father.[47]

References: (1) 2 Thessalonians 1:1; (2) 1 John 4:14; (3) John 15:5; (4) Philippians 4:13; (5) 1 Corinthians 1:30;

(6) 2 Corinthians 5:21; (7) Revelation 17:14;
(8) Revelation 19:16; (9) John 14:6; (10) 1 Timothy
2:5; (11) John 15:15; (12) Proverbs 18:24; (13) Romans
8:17; (14) 1 Corinthians 3:9; (15) John 15:1;
(16) John 10:7; (17) John 10:14; (18) Exodus 15:26;
(19) Mark 4:38; (20) Matthew 11:28; (21) 1 Peter 2:21;
(22) Hebrews 4:15; (23) Psalms 18:2; (24) Galatians
2:20; (25) John 8:12; (26) John 6:35; (27) Malachi
4:2; (28) Song of Solomon 2:1; (29) Revelation 22:16;
(30) Isaiah 9:6; (31) Isaiah 9:6; (32) Isaiah 9:6;
(33) Isaiah 9:6; (34) Romans 1:4; (35) Mark 9:31;
(36) Galatians 3:13; (37) Hebrews 2:10; (38) Acts 17:28;
(39) John 1:1; (40) Matthew 1:23; (41) Colossians
2:9; (42) Colossians 2:10; (43) Colossians 1:17;
(44) Colossians 2:3; (45) Revelation 22:13;
(46) Matthew 28:18; (47) Philippians 2:9-10.

Bible Prayer: Heavenly Father,[1] thank you
for sending Jesus to be my Savior.[2] He is my
life.[3] He is my wisdom, my sanctification, my
righteousness, and my redemption.[4] Thank
you for permitting me to be crucified with
Him. Even though I am crucified with Him, I
live through Him. He lives within me, and the
life I now live I live by faith in your Son, Father.
I love Him so much because He loves me and
He gave himself for me.[5] He is my Lord.[6] He
is my peace.[7] He is faithful, and He establishes
me and guards me from the evil one.[8] In the
name of Jesus,[9] Amen.

References: *(1) Luke 11:2; (2) 1 John 4:14; (3) John 14:6; (4) 1 Corinthians 1:30; (5) Galatians 2:20; (6) Romans 10:9-10; (7) Ephesians 2:14; (8) 2 Thessalonians 3:3; (9) John 15:16.*

Related Scriptures: *Luke 1:47; John 6:47; Acts 2:36; Romans 5:8; 1 Corinthians 13:13; 2 Corinthians 5:17; Philippians 3:9; Hebrews 12:2-3.*

31

MY JOY OVERFLOWS

Bible Promise: "Do not sorrow, for the joy of the Lord is your strength" (Neh. 8:10, NKJV).

Bible Meditation: My joy is made complete when I pray in the authority of Jesus' name[1] because I know that God, my Father, will hear and answer my prayers.[2] His abiding joy is my strength.[3] It is a joy that goes so much deeper than anything this world has to offer.[4] It is far more wonderful than any human emotion. Like a fountain that springs from the depths of the earth, the joy of the Lord bubbles up from my spirit and fills me; then it flows forth from my life and touches all those with whom I come in contact.[5]

This amazing joy comes as a gift to me from my heavenly Father who loves me with an everlasting love.[6] This fact, in itself, brings overwhelming joy to my heart. It is an inexpressible kind of joy; it is full of the glory of God.[7] God's joy enables me to rise above all the circumstances of my life and to stay on top.[8] The joy God gives to me is a fruit of His Spirit in my life.[9]

As I reflect on the joy He gives to me, I want to shout and sing.[10] The joy of the Lord leads me to praise Him and to rejoice evermore.[11] It is so abundant that it gives me a cheerful countenance and a merry heart that does me good like a medicine.[12]

As I experience the presence of God,[13] my heart is overcome with joy. He pours His joy upon me,[14] and it overflows in all areas of my life. It covers me and reaches out to others. How I rejoice in His marvelous love for me.[15]

The gladness and joy of God have overtaken me,[16] and I resolve to never be downcast again. I pray with joy, work with joy, and minister to others with the joy of the Lord. My heart literally leaps with excitement because my Father has anointed me with the oil of joy.[17] My joy is complete in Him, and everlasting joy will be my crown from henceforth and forevermore.[18]

The love of God is the source of all my joy and happiness.[19] I never knew true joy until I knew Him. There is nothing in this world that compares with the joy of the Lord. I receive His promise of joy and I determine to walk in His joy forever.[20]

References: (1) John 16:24; (2) John 16:23; (3) Nehemiah 8:10; (4) Psalms 43:4; (5) Isaiah 55:12; (6) Psalms 106:1; (7) 1 Peter 1:8; (8) Psalms 126; (9) Galatians 5:22; (10) Psalms 5:11; (11) 1 Thessalonians 5:16; (12) Proverbs 17:22; (13) Psalms 16:11; (14) Hebrews 1:9; (15) Ephesians 2:4; (16) Psalms 4:7;

(17) Psalms 45:7; (18) Psalms 103:4; (19) Psalms 43:4; (20) Isaiah 55:12.

Bible Prayer: Your joy, O Lord, bubbles up within my soul from the inner wellspring that comes from knowing you.[1] It floods my spirit, soul and body. It fills my mind with happiness.[2] I sing with joy[3] when I realize who you are, Father, and when I contemplate all you have done for me and mine, my excitement intensifies.[4] Thank you for joy.[5] You are my highest joy and my delight.[6] I will walk in the strength your joy gives to me,[7] and as I ask and receive in Jesus' name, I know my joy will be full.[8] Thank you, Lord. Amen.

References: (1) Isaiah 12:3; (2) Isaiah 61:7; (3) Psalms 67:4; (4) 1 Thessalonians 5:16; (5) 1 Thessalonians 5:18; (6) Psalms 43:4; (7) Nehemiah 8:10; (8) John 16:24.

Related Scriptures: Deuteronomy 16:15; Psalms 16:11; Psalms 28:7; Psalms 43:4; Psalms 45:7; Psalms 48:2; Isaiah 35:10; Philemon 7; 1 John 1:4.

KINGDOM

32

THE KINGDOM OF GOD IS WITHIN ME

Bible Promise: "The kingdom of God cometh not with observation: Neither shall they say, Lo here! or, lo there! for, behold, the kingdom of God is within you" (Luke 17:20-21).

Bible Meditation: Jesus Christ is the King of kings[1] and the Lord of lords.[2] Because He lives within me[3] I know that His kingdom is within me too.[4] His kingdom does not consist of meat and drink, but of righteousness, peace, and joy in the Holy Spirit.[5] I am the temple of the Holy Spirit and His holiness is within me.[6] I am Christ's, and Christ is God's.[7]

The Kingdom of God is always near me.[8] God has delivered me from the power of darkness and has translated me into the Kingdom of His dear Son, my Lord and Savior, Jesus Christ,[9] in whom I have redemption through His blood, even the forgiveness of my sins.[10] I will walk worthy of God who has called me unto His kingdom and His glory.[11] It is my heart's desire to be counted worthy of the Kingdom of God that is within me.[12]

The Lord will deliver me from every evil work, and He will preserve me unto His heavenly kingdom. To Him be glory forever and ever.[13] My heart fills with gratitude when I reflect on the fact that God, my Father, loves me. He has promised His kingdom to me. He chose me — a common person — to be rich in faith so that I would be able to inherit His kingdom.[14] It is my Father's good pleasure to give me the Kingdom.[15]

I have received His kingdom, and it cannot be shaken. He has given me the riches of His grace to enjoy. Therefore, I will serve and worship God with reverence and godly fear, because I know that He is truly a consuming fire.[16] He has given me entrance into His kingdom,[17] and His kingdom is within me.[18]

As I learn how to be poor in spirit, depending wholly upon God, I will experience more of the kingdom of heaven.[19] When I am persecuted for righteousness' sake the Kingdom of heaven is mine.[20] As I humble myself like a little child, I enjoy the kingdom in my life.[21] I will seek first God's kingdom, and His righteousness, and in so doing I know He will provide me with everything I need.[22]

References: (1) *Revelation 19:16;* (2) *Revelation 17:14;* (3) *Colossians 1:27;* (4) *Luke 17:21;* (5) *Romans 14:17;* (6) *1 Corinthians 6:19;* (7) *1 Corinthians 3:23;* (8) *Luke 10:11;* (9) *Colossians 1:13;* (10) *Colossians 1:14;*

(11) 1 Thessalonians 2:12; (12) 2 Thessalonians 1:5; (13) 2 Timothy 4:18; (14) James 2:5; (15) Luke 12:32; (16) Hebrews 12:28-29; (17) 2 Peter 1:11; (18) Luke 17:21; (19) Matthew 5:3; (20) Matthew 5:10; (21) Matthew 18:4; (22) Philippians 4:19.

Bible Prayer: My Father, you live in the Kingdom of heaven.[1] Your kingdom is coming,[2] and it has already come to be within me.[3] Let your peace rule in my heart, Lord.[4] Your name is holy, Father, and your kingdom has come. Let your will be done in my life and throughout the earth as it is done in heaven.[5] Give me this day my daily bread.[6] Forgive me of my sins in the same way that I forgive the sins of those who wrong me. I know you will never lead me into temptation, Lord, and you will always deliver me from evil.[7] These things are a part of my inheritance as your child, O King.[8] Thank you for everything you have done and are doing in my life.[9] I love you, Lord.[10] In Jesus' name I pray,[11] Amen.

References: *(1) Luke 11:2; (2) Luke 11:2; (3) Luke 17:21; (4) Colossians 3:15; (5) Luke 11:2; (6) Luke 11:3; (7) Luke 11:4; (8) John 1:12; (9) Psalms 107:1; (10) 1 John 4:21; (11) John 15:16.*

Related Scriptures: *Matthew 3:2; Matthew 12:28; Matthew 13:11; Matthew 22:2; Mark 12:34; Luke 7:28; Luke 12:31; 1 Corinthians 4:20.*

33

ETERNAL LIFE IS MINE

Bible Promise: "In My Father's house are many mansions; if it were not so, I would have told you. I go to prepare a place for you. And if I go and prepare a place for you, I will come again and receive you to Myself; that where I am, there you may be also" (John 14:2-3, NKJV).

Bible Meditation: God loves me[1] so much that He gave His only begotten Son to be a sacrifice for my sins.[2] By believing in Him I receive saving faith that leads to eternal life.[3] I believe that Jesus Christ died for me.[4] He is my Savior.[5] He is my Lord.[6] I am saved.[7] A crown of righteousness is laid up for me in heaven.[8]

Through God's abundant grace, faith was imparted to my heart.[9] I was born again.[10] I was adopted into the family of God,[11] and now my heart cries, "Abba, Father."[12] I became a new creation in Christ Jesus[13] as I drew living waters from His wells of salvation.[14]

Because I am now in Christ,[15] and He is in me,[16] everything in my life is new.[17] The old has passed away.[18] From now on, I know that goodness and mercy will follow me all the days of my life, and I will dwell in the house of the Lord forever.[19]

I am astounded as I realize that even now my Lord and Savior, Jesus Christ,[20] is preparing a place for me in heaven.[21] He wants me to live with Him forever! This knowledge thrills me.

When I get to heaven I will experience fullness of joy in the presence of the Lord.[22] At His right hand I will experience pleasures forevermore.[23]

This wonderful eternal life has already begun for me, and it will never end! Hallelujah! What a Savior! Hallelujah for His so-great salvation[24] which is for me.

References: *(1) 1 John 4:19; (2) John 3:16; (3) Acts 16:31; (4) Romans 5:8; (5) 2 Timothy 1:10; (6) Luke 24:34; (7) Romans 10:13; (8) James 1:12; (9) Ephesians 2:8-9; (10) John 3:7; (11) Galatians 4:5; (12) Galatians 4:6; (13) 2 Corinthians 5:17; (14) Isaiah 12:3; (15) Ephesians 2:10; (16) Colossians 1:27; (17) Romans 6:4; (18) 2 Corinthians 5:17; (19) Psalms 23:6; (20) 1 John 4:14; (21) John 14:3; (22) Psalms 16:11; (23) Psalms 16:11; (24) Hebrews 2:3.*

Bible Prayer: Lord, I thank you for the gift of eternal life.[1] You have shown me that the wages of sin are death,[2] but your superlative gift is a life that never ends.[3] Your promise of eternal life fills my heart with confidence,[4] love,[5] and assurance.[6] Heaven truly is my home,[7] and I look forward to living there with you, all my fellow-believers, members of my

family, my loved ones, and the angelic host.[8]
In Jesus' name I pray,[9] Amen.

References: *(1) Romans 6:23; (2) Romans 6:23;*
(3) 1 John 2:25; (4) Ephesians 3:12; (5) 1 John 4:8;
(6) 1 John 5:13; (7) John 14:2-3; (8) Revelation 14:10;
(9) John 15:16.

Related Scriptures: *Deuteronomy 33:27; Psalms*
16:11; Psalms 21:6; Daniel 4:3; Habakkuk 3:6;
Matthew 25:46; Mark 10:30; Luke 16:9; Luke 18:30;
John 3:15-16; John 3:36; John 4:14; John 10:28;
Romans 6:23; 2 Corinthians 5:1; Galatians 6:8;
1 Timothy 1:16; 1 John 5:11; Jude 21.

34

THE LORD IS MY LIGHT AND MY SALVATION

Bible Promise: "The Lord is my light and my salvation; Whom shall I fear? The Lord is the strength of my life; Of whom shall I be afraid" (Ps. 27:1, NKJV).

Bible Meditation: The Lord is my light.[1] I will walk in His light.[2] He is the Light of life.[3] His Word is a lamp unto my feet and a light unto my path.[4] I trust in Him with all my heart, not leaning unto my own understanding. In all my ways I will acknowledge Him as the Light of my life, and I know He will direct my paths.[5]

Because He is my light and my salvation I will not fear anyone or anything.[6] Though a host encamp against me, my heart shall not fear.[7] God's love and light make me confident.[8] The important thing is to realize that I will dwell in the house of the Lord all the days of my life.[9] I will dwell in His house forever,[10] and goodness and mercy will follow me always.[11]

My heavenly Father lifts the light of His countenance upon me.[12] He puts gladness into my heart.[13] In Him there is a fountain of life; in His light I see light.[14] He has taken me out of the kingdom of darkness into His marvelous light.[15] He has saved me[16] and made me whole.[17]

He will light my candle in the darkness.[18] My spirit is the candle of the Lord.[19] The entrance of His words gives light to my soul and spirit.[20] Even the night shall be light about me.[21] In Christ, the darkness and the light are both alike.[22]

The Lord is a light unto me.[23] God is light; in Him there is no darkness at all.[24] I will walk in the light as He is in the light. This will enable me to have fellowship with other believers because the blood of Jesus Christ cleanses me from all sin.[25] It is this cleansing that enables me to walk in the light.[26]

References: (1) Psalms 27:1; (2)1 John 1:7; (3) John 1:9; (4) Psalms 119:105; (5) Proverbs 3:5-6; (6) Psalms 27:1; (7) Psalms 27:3; (8) Psalms 27:3; (9) Psalms 27:4; (10) Psalms 27:4; (11) Psalms 23:6; (12) Psalms 4:6; (13) Psalms 4:7; (14) Psalms 36:9; (15) 1 Peter 2:9; (16) James 1:21; (17) Matthew 9:22; (18) Psalms 18:28; (19) Proverbs 20:27; (20) Psalms 119:130; (21) Psalms 139:11; (22) Psalms 139:12; (23) 1 John 1:5; (24) 1 John 1:5; (25) 1 John 1:7; (26) 1 John 1:6.

Bible Prayer: Lord, you are my light.[1] Your light shines in the darkness.[2] You are the true light that lights those who believe in you.[3] All things were made by you, and your life is my light.[4] I thank you and praise you for being the

Light of the world.[5] I will follow you, and you will never permit me to walk in darkness again.[6] You have given me the light of life.[7] Thank you for taking me out of the kingdom of darkness into your marvelous light.[8] In Jesus' name I pray,[9] Amen.

References: (1) John 1:4; (2) John 1:5; (3) John 1:9; (4) John 1:4; (5) John 8:12; (6) John 8:12; (7) John 8:12; (8) 1 Peter 2:9; (9) John 15:16.

Related Scriptures: Genesis 1:3; Psalms 89:15; Proverbs 6:23; Matthew 4:16; John 9:5; Ephesians 5:8; Ephesians 5:14; 1 John 2:10.

35

GOD LOVES ME!

Bible Promise: "And hope does not disappoint us, because God has poured out his love into our hearts by the Holy Spirit, whom he has given us" (Rom. 5:5, NIV).

Bible Meditation: God loves me![1] This is the greatest truth in the entire universe. His love sets me free.[2] His love helps me to love myself and others.[3] I love God because He first loved me.[4] His lovingkindness is better than life to me.[5] His love is stronger than death.[6]

God loved me so much that He sent His only begotten Son to live and die for me so that I would be able to live with Him forever in heaven.[7] Through His love I have abundant life here on earth as well.[8] Nothing will ever be able to separate me from the love of God in Christ Jesus, my Lord.[9]

There is no greater love than that which Jesus demonstrated by dying on the cross.[10] He who knew no sin became sin for me so that the righteousness of God would be imparted to me.[11] While I was yet a sinner, the Lord Jesus died for me.[12]

It was God's love for me that drew me to Jesus in the first place.[13] He is showing me how to return His love so that I might learn to love Him with all my heart, mind, soul, and strength.[14] He is love,[15] and His Spirit empowers me to love others as I love myself.[16]

The love of God fills my heart to overflowing because His Spirit dwells within me.[17] His love is deeper than the mighty oceans, and it is broader than the universe. The length and depth and width and height of God's amazing love are truly beyond measure.[18]

The beautiful love of God enables me to be a fruit-bearing Christian in all the relationships and responsibilities of my life.[19] As I reflect on God's love for me, I feel washed, bathed, immersed, and anointed with liquid love that fills me with warmth, assurance, and peace. I will walk in His love throughout this day.[20]

References: (1) 1 John 3:1; (2) Romans 8:1-2; (3) Matthew 22:37-39; (4) 1 John 4:19; (5) Psalms 63:3; (6) Song of Solomon 8:6; (7) John 3:16; (8) John 10:10; (9) Romans 8:38-39; (10) John 15:13; (11) 2 Corinthians 5:21; (12) Romans 5:8; (13) Song of Solomon 2:4; (14) Matthew 22:37; (15) 1 John 4:8; (16) Romans 5:5; (17) Galatians 5:22; (18) Ephesians 3:18; (19) John 15:8-9; (20) Ephesians 5:2.

Bible Prayer: Father, thank you for your love.[1] I love you so much, and I want to learn to love you with all my heart, soul, mind, and strength.[2] Wean me from other interests that take so much of my time, energy, and attention, and help me to keep my focus on you throughout this day.[3] Clothe me with your love as you pour it forth in my heart and life. Let your Spirit's love flow out to others throughout this day, Lord.[4]

Thank you for sending your Son, my Lord and Savior, Jesus Christ, to live and die for me.[5] Help me to remember that His central message was and is love, and everything He did and does stems from His deep and permeating love.[6] Thank you for loving me so much.[7] Because you have received me,[8] chosen me,[9] and accepted me,[10] I am learning how to accept myself and even to love myself in a healthy way.[11]

As I respond to your love, Father, it gives me a renewed sense of purpose,[12] and it leads me to victory in all that I do.[13] By the enabling power and anointing of your Spirit I will walk in love throughout this day.[14] Thank you, Father. In Jesus' name I pray,[15] Amen.

References: *(1) Proverbs 8:17; (2) Matthew 22:37; (3) Isaiah 26:3; (4) Galatians 5:22; (5) John 3:16; (6) 1 John 4:7-12; (7) Ephesians 3:17-19; (8) Romans 15:7; (9) John 15:16; (10) Ezekiel 43:27; (11) Matthew 22:39; (12) John 15:12; (13) Romans 8:37; (14) Ephesians 5:2; (15) John 16:23.*

Related Scriptures: *Deuteronomy 6:5; 2 Chronicles 5:13; Psalms 13:5; Psalms 31:7; Psalms 52:8; Psalms 106:1; Isaiah 63:9; Lamentations 3:32; Joel 2:13; 1 Corinthians 13; 2 Corinthians 5:14; Galatians 5:6; Ephesians 2:4; Philippians 1:9; 1 Thessalonians 3:12; 1 John 4:7-21.*

36

I WALK IN LOVE

Bible Promise: "My command is this: Love each other as I have loved you. Greater love has no one than this, that he lay down his life for his friends" (John 15:12-13, NIV).

Bible Meditation: If I speak in the tongues of men and of angels, but have not love, I am only a resounding gong or a clanging cymbal.[1] I choose to walk in love,[2] to speak the truth in love,[3] to receive others as Jesus has received me,[4] to bear the fruit of love in all the relationships of my life,[5] to let my faith be expressed through love,[6] to love God with all my heart, soul, mind, and strength,[7] and to love my neighbor as I love myself.[8]

In love, I will honor others.[9] I will always endeavor to love without hypocrisy.[10] God's love for me compels me to love others[11] as I realize that His love is poured into my heart by the Holy Spirit.[12] I know that love is of God, and everyone who loves knows God.[13] I will be a person of love at all times, one who is constantly walking in love.

God is love.[14] His perfect love casts out all fear from my heart.[15] Nothing shall ever separate me from His love.[16] If I do not have

love I do not have anything.[17] Love is patient
and kind. It does not envy; it does not boast; it
is not proud.[18] Love is not rude; it is never self-
seeking; it is not easily angered; and it keeps no
record of wrongs.[19] Love rejoices in the truth,
and it never delights in evil.[20] Love always
protects, trusts, hopes, and perseveres.[21]

Love never fails.[22] These three remain:
faith, hope, and love, but the greatest of these
is love.[23] I will walk in love throughout this
day because I know that love is the more
excellent way.[24]

References: (1) *1 Corinthians 13:1; (2) 1 John 2:6;
(3) Ephesians 4:15; (4) Romans 15:7; (5) Galatians
5:22; (6) Galatians 5:6; (7) Matthew 22:37;
(8) Matthew 22:39; (9) Romans 12:10; (10) Romans
12:9; (11) 2 Corinthians 5:14; (12) Romans 5:5;
(13) 1 John 4:7; (14) 1 John 4:8; (15) 1 John 4:18;
(16) Romans 8:38-39; (17) 1 Corinthians 13:2;
(18) 1 Corinthians 13:4; (19) 1 Corinthians 13:5;
(20) 1 Corinthians 13:6; (21) 1 Corinthians 13:7;
(22) 1 Corinthians 13:8; (23) 1 Corinthians 13:13;
(24) 1 Corinthians 12:31.*

Bible Prayer: Heavenly Father,[1] I love you with
all my heart, mind, soul, and strength.[2] I praise
you[3] for commending your love toward me in
that while I was yet a sinner Jesus Christ died for
me.[4] You are love itself.[5] Continuously fill me
with your Spirit,[6] Lord, so that I will be able

to produce the fruit of your Spirit[7] in all the relationships and responsibilities of my life. Thank you for placing your banner of love[8] over me, for casting out all my fear,[9] and for giving me a spirit of love, peace, and a sound mind.[10] I love you, Father, and I know you love me.[11] In Jesus' name[12] I pray, Amen.

References: *(1) John 5:17; (2) Matthew 22:37; (3) Psalms 119:171; (4) Romans 5:8; (5) 1 John 4:8; (6) Ephesians 5:18; (7) Galatians 5:22; (8) Song of Solomon 2:4; (9) 1 John 4:18; (10) 2 Timothy 1:7; (11) John 3:16; (12) John 15:16.*

Related Scriptures: *Matthew 5:44; Mark 12:30; Luke 10:27; Romans 12:10; 1 Corinthians 2:9; Galatians 5:13; 1 Thessalonians 3:12; Hebrews 13:1; 1 Peter 2:17; 2 John 6.*

PATIENCE

37

I WALK IN PATIENCE

Bible Promise: "Wait on the Lord; Be of good courage, And He shall strengthen your heart; Wait, I say, on the Lord!" (Ps. 27:14, NKJV).

Bible Meditation: One fruit of God's Holy Spirit in my life is patience.[1] It is trusting in Him with all my heart that enables me to be patient.[2] I will trust Him with all my heart and lean not unto my own understanding. In all my ways I will acknowledge Him, and I know He will direct my paths.[3]

God has promised me that I may enter into His rest.[4] His Son, my Lord and Savior, Jesus Christ, has invited me to come unto Him when I am weary, and He has promised me His rest when I do so.[5] I realize that there are at least three things that prevent me from finding His rest, and they are disobedience, hardheartedness, and a lack of faith.[6] I choose to obey the Lord,[7] to keep my heart open and pure,[8] and to walk in faith at all times.[9] It is the trying of my faith that works patience into me.[10]

I want patience to have its perfect work in me so that I will be made perfect and entire, wanting nothing.[11] When this happens I will be able to rest in the Lord, to wait patiently for

Him. There will be no worry, anger, or evil in my life because I have learned to wait on the Lord. The Lord promises me that the exercise of patience in my life will enable me to inherit the earth.[12]

Every time I wait patiently for the Lord, He inclines unto me, and He hears my cry. It is He who brought me out of the dismal pit filled with miry clay, and it is He who set my feet upon the rock of His Word and established my goings. He has put a new song in my mouth, even praise to my God. Many will see and hear my new song of praise and they will trust in the Lord.[13]

By waiting on the Lord patience grows in my heart. My strength is renewed and I am able to mount up with wings as eagles do. It is patience that enables me to run and not be weary, to walk and not faint.[14] All my hope is in the Lord. He delivers me from all my transgressions and fears.[15]

I choose to walk in patience because I know the Lord will come through for me.[16] With all diligence, therefore, I will build my life on faith, and I will add virtue, knowledge, temperance, patience, godliness, brotherly kindness, and love to my faith.[17] I will let these qualities abound within me so that I will be fruitful in the knowledge of my Lord Jesus Christ.[18]

References: (1) Galatians 5:22; (2) Proverbs 3:5;
(3) Proverbs 3:5-6; (4) Hebrews 4:1; (5) Matthew
11:28; (6) Hebrews 4; (7) Acts 5:29; (8) Matthew 5:8;
(9) 2 Corinthians 5:7; (10) James 1:3; (11) James 1:4;
(12) Psalms 37:7-9; (13) Psalms 40:1-3; (14) Isaiah
40:31; (15) Psalms 39:7-8; (16) Isaiah 25:9;
(17) 2 Peter 1:5-7; (18) 2 Peter 1:8.

Bible Prayer: Heavenly Father, I love you.[1] In
the patience you provide for me I will hold fast
the profession of my faith without wavering,
because I know you are faithful to me.[2] I will
wait on you continually.[3] You are my God, and
every time I've waited in patience before you,
you have come through. Therefore, my heart is
filled with gladness and I rejoice in your salvation.[4] You always pick me up when I fall and
you lift me when I feel overwrought.[5] Show
me your ways, O Lord. Teach me your paths.
Lead me in your truth, and teach me. You are
the God of my salvation, and it pleases me to
be able to wait on you all day long. Your integrity
and uprightness will preserve me because I
wait on you.[6] In Jesus' name I pray,[7] Amen.

References: (1) 1 John 5:2; (2) Hebrews 10:23;
(3) Hosea 12:6; (4) Isaiah 25:9; (5) Psalms 145:14-15;
(6) Psalms 25:21; (7) John 15:16.

Related Scriptures: Luke 8:15; Luke 21:19; Romans
5:3-4; Romans 8:25; Colossians 1:11; Hebrews 6:12.

38

I HAVE PEACE

Bible Promise: "And the peace of God, which surpasses all understanding, will guard your hearts and minds through Christ Jesus" (Phil. 4:7, NKJV).

Bible Meditation: God cares about me.[1] Because He does I am able to cast all my cares upon Him.[2] He has promised to meet all my needs according to His riches in glory.[3] I will rejoice in the Lord always.[4] I will be anxious about nothing; instead of worrying, I will let my requests and needs be made known to my Father in prayer.[5] Through prayer and supplication, with thanksgiving, I know all my needs will be met.[6] God, my loving Father, knows everything I need.[7] He never forsakes the righteous.[8]

These are facts of my faith. They are a sure foundation on which to build my life.[9] Even when the winds and floods assail, I can stand secure in God and His Word.[10] There is nothing to fear because my Father loves me.[11] The peace of God that surpasses all understanding will keep my heart and mind through Christ Jesus.[12]

In quietness and in confidence I will find strength.[13] My Father will keep me in perfect peace as I keep my mind focused on Him and as I trust completely in Him.[14] God has given me a spirit of love and peace instead of a spirit of fear and this keeps my mind sound and clear.[15] There is no fear in His marvelous love.[16]

The Lord Jesus Christ is my peace.[17] Through Him I have access in the Spirit to my loving Father in heaven.[18] I have peace with God through the blood of Christ.[19] This knowledge gives me confidence to approach the Father's throne where I know I will receive mercy and grace to help in my time of need.[20] I will never cast away my confidence in Him.[21]

I will seek first the Kingdom of God and His righteousness, knowing that as I do so, my Father will supply all my needs.[22] I will take no anxious thought, therefore, about the future,[23] because I know that God will be there with me.[24] My Father holds the future in His mighty hands and He watches over His Word to see that it comes to pass in my life.[25]

References: (1) 1 Peter 5:7; (2) 1 Peter 5:7;
(3) Philippians 4:19; (4) Philippians 4:4; (5) Philippians 4:6; (6) Philippians 4:6; (7) Matthew 6:8;
(8) Psalms 37:25; (9) 2 Timothy 2:19; (10) Matthew 7:25-27; (11) 1 John 4:18; (12) Philippians 4:7;
(13) Isaiah 30:15; (14) Isaiah 26:3; (15) 2 Timothy 1:7; (16) 1 John 4:18; (17) Ephesians 2:14;
(18) Ephesians 2:18; (19) Colossians 1:20;

(20) Hebrews 4:16; (21) Hebrews 10:35; (22) Matthew 6:33; (23) Matthew 6:34; (24) Hebrews 13:5; (25) Jeremiah 1:12.

Bible Prayer: Father, because I know you love me,[1] I will not let my heart be troubled.[2] I believe in you, and I believe in your Son, my Lord and Savior, Jesus Christ.[3] I know that I will have a home with you in heaven forever.[4] I thank you for the certainty that when I ask anything in Jesus' name you will do it for me.[5] I love you and I will keep your commandments.[6]

You have given me the Comforter, your precious Holy Spirit, to abide with me forever.[7] He is the Spirit of Truth,[8] and His presence gives great comfort to my life.[9] I receive your promise of peace as I pray.[10] Thank you for giving me your peace, Lord.[11] Because I have your peace I will never again be worried or afraid.[12] In Jesus' name,[13] I pray, Amen.

References: (1) 1 John 4:19; (2) John 14:1; (3) John 14:1; (4) John 14:2; (5) John 14:14; (6) John 14:15; (7) John 14:16; (8) John 14:17; (9) John 14:18; (10) John 14:27; (11) John 14:27; (12) John 14:27; (13) John 15:16.

Related Scriptures: Psalms 4:8; Psalms 29:11; Psalms 119:165; Proverbs 3:2; Philippians 4:9; 1 Thessalonians 5:23; Hebrews 13:20.

POSSIBILITIES

39

ALL THINGS ARE POSSIBLE WITH GOD

Bible Promise: "With men this is impossible; but with God all things are possible" (Matt. 19:26).

Bible Meditation: Nothing is too hard for my Father in heaven.[1] He can fix anything.[2] The truth is, He can do anything but fail.[3] I put my faith in Him,[4] not in myself or in any other human being, not in vain philosophies, or any system of this earth.

My God is able to do exceedingly abundantly beyond all I can ask or think.[5] He is omnipotent (all-powerful),[6] omniscient (all-knowing),[7] and omnipresent (present everywhere).[8] He is the King of kings and the Lord of lords,[9] and He loves me.[10]

I join my faith to His power, realizing that I can do all things through Christ who strengthens me.[11] Through the power of His Spirit I am more than a conqueror.[12]

I am strengthened with all His power.[13] God is a miracle-worker.[14] His Son, my Lord and Savior, Jesus Christ, is the Great Physician who healed all who came to Him.[15] There is no mountain too high, no tunnel too deep, no valley so dark that will keep my God from prevailing. He has already won my battles.[16] Satan is a defeated foe.[17]

The Lord has clothed me with His power from on high.[18] Power and might are in my Father's hands.[19] His power and glory go beyond the comprehension of my mind. His arm is endued with power.[20] He formed the earth, and He formed me through His creative power.[21]

My Father's ability is beyond all measurement.[22] It is all-surpassing, and I want Him to have the preeminence in all that I say, think, and do.[23] His power works in me;[24] it strengthens me and enables me to do whatever He asks me to do.[25]

I live by the power of my God.[26] The power of His resurrection has set me free from the law of sin and death.[27] How I praise Him that I no longer have the spirit of fear, but of power, love, and a sound mind.[28] I believe my Father can do anything, and He has proven this to me in abundant ways and means.[29] I will walk in His enabling power throughout this day.[30]

References: (1) *Genesis 18:14;* (2) *Mark 10:27;* (3) *Matthew 19:26;* (4) *Acts 27:25;* (5) *Ephesians 3:20;* (6) *Matthew 28:18;* (7) *Psalms 139:2-4;* (8) *Psalms 139:7-10;* (9) *Revelation 19:16;*

(10) John 3:16; (11) Philippians 4:13; (12) Romans 8:37; (13) 2 Corinthians 13:4; (14) Psalms 62:11; (15) Luke 9:11; (16) Psalms 24:8; (17) Colossians 2:15; (18) Luke 24:49; (19) Psalms 18:35; (20) Psalms 89:13; (21) Psalms 139:13-16; (22) Psalms 147:5; (23) Colossians 1:18; (24) Ephesians 3:20; (25) Ephesians 3:16; (26) 2 Corinthians 13:4; (27) Romans 8:2; (28) 2 Timothy 1:7; (29) Jeremiah 33:3; (30) 1 Peter 1:5.

Bible Prayer: Thank you, Father, for your power.[1] I believe in you,[2] and I know that all things are possible to me through faith.[3] I claim your promise of power now,[4] Lord, and even as I do so, I sense your strength[5] pouring into me. How I love[6] and praise you[7] for the fact that you love me,[8] and this realization fills me with the confidence[9] that comes from knowing that all things are possible through you.[10] In Jesus' name I pray,[11] Amen.

References: *(1) 2 Corinthians 4:7; (2) Galatians 2:16; (3) Mark 9:23; (4) Acts 1:8; (5) Psalms 43:2; (6) 1 John 4:19; (7) Psalms 42:11; (8) 1 John 4:8; (9) Isaiah 30:15; (10) Matthew 19:26; (11) John 15:16.*

Related Scriptures: *Exodus 15:6; 1 Samuel 10:6; 2 Chronicles 20:6; Psalms 20:6; Psalms 66:3; Psalms 89:13; Psalms 147:5; Jeremiah 10:12; Zechariah 4:6; Luke 24:49; 2 Corinthians 4:7; Ephesians 6:10; Revelation 19:1.*

40

THERE'S A NEW SONG IN MY HEART

Bible Promise: "He put a new song in my mouth, a hymn of praise to our God. Many will see and fear and put their trust in the Lord" (Ps. 40:3, NIV).

Bible Meditation: The Lord is my light and my salvation;[1] He is my strength and my song.[2] With the song of my mouth I will praise Him.[3] I will sing unto Him a new song.[4] In the day and in the night His song will be with me.[5]

I will sing unto the Lord and bless His name. I will show forth His salvation from day to day.[6] I will declare His glory and His wonders among all the people.[7] This is the new song He has given to me. The Lord is great and greatly to be praised.[8] He is to be feared above all gods.[9]

My Lord made the heavens and the earth.[10] Honor and majesty are before Him. Strength and beauty are in His sanctuary.[11] I will give unto the Lord the glory that is due to His name.[12] I will go into His courts with thanksgiving, honor, praise, and song.[13] I will worship the Lord in the beauty of His holiness.[14]

The Lord reigns.[15] He is the Lord of lords and the King of kings.[16] He is my God, and I will ever honor, adore, and praise Him with the song of my lips.[17] The words of my song of praise will honor the Lamb of God who was slain for me.[18] I will sing of the power of His blood that has washed me clean.[19] He has made me a king and priest unto God. I will reign on the earth[20] and with Him in heaven.[21]

Worthy is the Lamb that was slain to receive power, and riches, and wisdom, and strength, and honour, and glory, and blessing.[22] Blessing and honor and glory and power be unto Him who sits on the throne, and unto the Lamb forever and ever.[23] He is the object of my worship, my love, my all.

References: (1) Psalms 27:1; (2) Exodus 15:2; (3) Psalms 68:4; (4) Psalms 33:3; (5) Psalms 42:8; (6) Psalms 96:2; (7) Psalms 96:3; (8) Psalms 48:1; (9) Psalms 96:4; (10) Genesis 1; (11) Psalms 96:6; (12) Psalms 96:8; (13) Psalms 100:4; (14) Psalms 96:9; (15) Psalms 99:1; (16) 1 Timothy 6:15; (17) Psalms 118:28; (18) Revelation 5:12; (19) Revelation 5:9; (20) Revelation 5:10; (21) Revelation 20:6; (22) Revelation 5:12; (23) Revelation 5:13.

Bible Prayer: Lord,[1] you are my strength and my salvation.[2] I praise you with the new song you have given to me.[3] I worship and honor you for who you are.[4] I thank you for all you have done for me.[5] You have redeemed me,[6] and I will sing of your redemption throughout my life.[7] I am not my own because I have been bought by the blood that your Son shed for my salvation.[8] I know that Jesus Christ is my Lord[9] and Savior,[10] and He is the Way, the Truth, and the Life.[11] I thank you, Father, that His death and resurrection enable me to have fellowship with you,[12] and I praise you that I will be able to reign with you and Him forever.[13] In Jesus' name[14] I pray, Amen.

References: *(1) Daniel 9:19; (2) Psalms 140:7; (3) Psalms 40:3; (4) Revelation 4:10; (5) Psalms 50:14; (6) Galatians 3:13; (7) Psalms 107:2; (8) 1 Corinthians 6:20; (9) 2 Peter 1:11; (10) 2 Timothy 1:10; (11) John 14:6; (12) 1 Timothy 2:5; (13) 2 Timothy 2:12; (14) John 15:16.*

Related Scriptures: *Psalms 7:17; Psalms 51:14; Psalms 68:4; Psalms 105:2; Proverbs 29:6; Isaiah 51:11.*

P R A I S E

41

GOD INHABITS MY PRAISES

Bible Promise: "But You are holy, enthroned in the praises of Israel" (Ps. 22:3, NKJV).

Bible Meditation: I will praise the Lord because His lovingkindness is better than life to me.[1] I will bless Him and lift up my hands in His name.[2] As I praise the Lord, my soul will be satisfied and I will praise Him with joyful lips.[3] Great is the Lord, and He is greatly to be praised.[4]

I will bless the Lord at all times, and His praise shall continually be in my mouth.[5] I will magnify the Lord and exalt His name.[6] I will enter His gates with thanksgiving and go into His courts with praise.[7] I will be thankful to him and I will bless His name because He is good and His mercy is everlasting. His truth endures to all generations.[8] The Lord is God. He made me. I am His child and a sheep in His pasture;[9] therefore, I will make a joyful noise unto Him,[10] I will serve Him with gladness,[11] and I will enter His presence with singing.[12]

I will bless the Lord with all that is within me.[13] I will never forget His benefits and blessings in my life.[14] He forgives all my iniquities and

He heals all my diseases.[15] He has redeemed my life from destruction, and He has crowned me with lovingkindness and tender mercies.[16] He satisfies my mouth with good things and renews my youth.[17]

As I offer praise to the Lord I glorify Him.[18] He has called me to show forth His praises by the way I live, because He called me out of darkness into His marvelous light.[19] I will live a life of praise before Him — in His sanctuary and in the firmament of His power.[20] I will praise Him for His mighty acts according to His excellent greatness.[21] I will bless His name from this time forth and forever more.[22] From the sunrise to the sunset I will praise the name of the Lord,[23] because I know that when I draw near to Him in prayer and praise, He will draw near to me.[24] God dwells in the atmosphere of praise,[25] and because I believe in Him He promises that rivers of living water will flow forth from me.[26]

References: (1) Psalms 63:3; (2) Psalms 63:4; (3) Psalms 63:5; (4) Psalms 48:1; (5) Psalms 34:1; (6) Psalms 34:3; (7) Psalms 100:4; (8) Psalms 100:5; (9) Psalms 100:3; (10) Psalms 100:1; (11) Psalms 100:2; (12) Psalms 100:2; (13) Psalms 103:1; (14) Psalms 103:2; (15) Psalms 103:3; (16) Psalms 103:4; (17) Psalms 103:5; (18) Psalms 50:23; (19) 1 Peter 2:9; (20) Psalms 150:1; (21) Psalms

150:2; (22) *Psalms* 113:2; (23) *Psalms* 113:3;
(24) *James* 4:8; (25) *Psalms* 22:3; (26) *John* 7:38.

Bible Prayer: O Lord, my God,[1] I praise you,[2] glorify you,[3] bless you,[4] honor you,[5] thank you,[6] magnify you,[7] and worship you.[8] You alone are worthy to receive glory, honor, and power, O Lord, for you created all things, and everything was created for your pleasure.[9]

It is a good thing to give thanks to you and to sing praise to your name, O Most High.[10] I will show forth your lovingkindness in the morning, and your faithfulness every night.[11] O Lord, your works are so great and your thoughts are very deep.[12] I will extol your name, O God, my King, and I will bless your name forever.[13] Every day I will bless you, and I will praise your name forever.[14]

You are so great, Father. Truly your greatness is unsearchable.[15] You are gracious, full of compassion, slow to anger, and of great mercy.[16] You are good to me, and your tender mercies are over all your works.[17] Thank you for being present in my praises, Lord.[18] I love you with all my heart, soul, mind and strength,[19] and I will praise you forevermore.[20] In Jesus' name I pray,[21] Amen.

References: (1) *Hosea* 14:1; (2) *Psalms* 65:1; (3) *Psalms* 86:12; (4) *Psalms* 16:7; (5) *Proverbs* 3:9; (6) *Philippians* 4:6; (7) *Psalms* 34:3; (8) *Revelation*

7:12; *(9) Revelation 4:11; (10) Psalms 92:1;*
(11) Psalms 92:2; (12) Psalms 92:5; (13) Psalms
145:1; (14) Psalms 145:2; (15) Psalms 145:3;
(16) Psalms 145:8; (17) Psalms 145:9; (18) Psalms
22:3; (19) Mark 12:30; (20) Psalms 145:1;
(21) John 16:23.

Related Scriptures: *Psalms 35:18; Psalms 40:8;*
Psalms 106:1; Isaiah 12:1; Jeremiah 20:13; Romans
15:11; Hebrews 13:15.

PRAYER

42

GOD HEARS MY PRAYERS

Bible Promise: "Now this is the confidence that we have in Him, that if we ask anything according to His will, He hears us" (1 John 5:14, NKJV).

Bible Meditation: God hears my prayers.[1] He wants me to pray to Him.[2] He recognizes my voice.[3] Through prayer I receive all He has for me.[4] The Father is calling me to prayer because He wants to have fellowship with me.[5] Through prayer I am able to express my reverence and adoration for Him who is my Father in heaven.[6]

When Jesus taught His disciples to pray, He reminded them of their need to pray daily.[7] He always exemplified this, and He continues to make intercession for me at the Father's right hand.[8]

Like my Lord and Savior, I want to cultivate a life of prayer, to pray without ceasing.[9] It is my heart-felt desire to learn how to discern God's voice when He speaks to me.[10] Through prayer this discernment will come. God's still, small voice will speak to me.[11]

Jesus is my Good Shepherd.[12] He knows me.[13] He loves me.[14] He takes good care of me.[15] I feel safe as His sheep, and even as He knows His sheep when they cry to Him, I want to be able to hear and know His voice as He speaks to me.[16]

Prayer is such a wonderful privilege. It is my direct access to the King of kings and the Lord of lords.[17] Through prayer I learn how to worship my Father in heaven who is worthy to receive honor, praise, and glory.[18] As I confess my sins to Him, I know He hears me, forgives me, and cleanses me from all unrighteousness.[19]

The prayer of thanksgiving leads me to rejoice in all He has done for me.[20] It enables me to enter into the throne-room of God.[21] The prayer of supplication assures me that my Father will meet all my needs.[22]

God hears me when I pray.[23] He recognizes my voice and He responds to my cry.[24] His prayer-promises cannot fail.[25] He is only a prayer away.[26] Because I know He hears me, full confidence floods my being, and I am able to approach His throne with conviction and certainty, knowing that when I do so, I will receive the grace and mercy I need in every given situation.[27] God hears my prayer, and He wants me to pray to Him.

References: *(1) Psalms 34:17; (2) Matthew 26:41;*
(3) John 10:14; (4) Matthew 21:22; (5) 1 Thessalonians
5:17; (6) Luke 11:2; (7) Matthew 26:41; (8) Hebrews 7:25;
(9) 1 Thessalonians 5:17; (10) John 10:4; (11) 1 Kings
19:12; (12) John 10:11; (13) Psalms 139:23;
(14) John 3:16; (15) 1 Peter 5:7; (16) Psalms 29:4;
(17) Revelation 19:16; (18) Revelation 4:11;
(19) 1 John 1:9; (20) 1 Thessalonians 5:18; (21) Psalms
100:4; (22) Philippians 4:19; (23) Psalms 66:19;
(24) Psalms 34:17; (25) 2 Corinthians 1:20;
(26) Jeremiah 33:3; (27) Hebrews 4:16.

Bible Prayer: Heavenly Father,[1] I have great
confidence in you.[2] I know you hear my
prayers.[3] You are listening to me even now. I
just want to take this opportunity to thank you
for your listening ear,[4] for accepting my cry,[5]
and for recognizing my voice.[6]

How I praise you for the fact that you
know what I need even before I express it to
you,[7] but you want me to express my needs to
you because you love to hear my voice and
you want to have fellowship with me.[8] You
are my Beloved,[9] Lord; I thank you that you are
mine, and I am yours.[10] In Jesus' name I pray,[11]
Amen.

References: *(1) Colossians 3:17; (2) Psalms 118:8-9;*
(3) Psalms 4:3; (4) Psalms 55:1; (5) Psalms 18:6;
(6) Psalms 77:1; (7) Matthew 6:8; (8) John 10:14;

(9) Song of Solomon 2:10; (10) Song of Solomon 2:16; (11) John 15:16.

Related Scriptures: *Deuteronomy 4:7; 2 Chronicles 7:14; 2 Chronicles 30:27; Psalms 4:1; Psalms 6:9; Psalms 17:1; Psalms 17:6; Psalms 65:2; Psalms 86:6; Proverbs 15:29; Matthew 6:5-14; Acts 10:31; 1 Peter 3:12.*

PRAYER

43

GOD ANSWERS MY PRAYERS

Bible Promise: "Call to Me, and I will answer you, and show you great and mighty things, which you do not know" (Jer. 33:3, NKJV).

Bible Meditation: God hears and answers my prayers.[1] I delight myself in Him[2] and He gives me the desires of my heart.[3] As I pray according to His will, He grants my petitions.[4] My heavenly Father knows what I need,[5] and He meets my every need faithfully and lovingly.[6] He supplies all my needs according to His riches in glory.[7]

When I ask, God gives His special answers to me. When I pray according to His plan, He responds to my prayers. He always rewards my faith.[8] When I knock, He opens the door; when I seek, He leads me.[9] He is such a great and good God.[10]

I will abide in Christ,[11] and I will let His words abide in me.[12] This abiding opens the door to all God has for me, and He will give me whatever I ask of Him.[13] My Father wants my joy to be full,[14] and so He gives me the authority of the Name of Jesus which fills me with joy and leads me to victory.[15] Praying in His name brings answers to my prayers.[16]

God wants to give me every good and perfect gift.[17] He lavishes His love upon me by inviting me into His banqueting hall.[18] His banner over me is love.[19] He has prepared a table for me, and He fills my cup to overflowing.[20] He always gives me my daily bread.[21]

I am drawing near to Him now, and as I do so, He draws near to me.[22] I will always pray in faith because I know from God's Word that He loves believing prayers, and He is committed to answering them.[23] My Father is a Rewarder of all who come to Him in faith.[24] I believe in Him,[25] and I look forward to all the rewards He has for me.[26] When I pray, I express faith to Him, fully expecting His hand to move.[27]

God answers my prayers because He loves me.[28] This leads me to trust in Him with all my heart, leaning not upon my own understanding. In all my ways I will acknowledge Him, and I know He will direct my paths.[29]

References: (1) *Psalms 28:6; (2) Psalms 37:4;*
(3) Psalms 37:4; (4) 1 John 5:14; (5) Matthew 6:8;
(6) Lamentations 3:23; (7) Philippians 4:19;
(8) Hebrews 11:6; (9) Matthew 7:8; (10) Isaiah 12:6;
(11) John 15:4; (12) John 15:7; (13) John 15:7;
(14) John 16:24; (15) John 16:23; (16) John 16:23;
(17) James 1:17; (18) Song of Solomon 2:4;

(19) Song of Solomon 2:4; (20) Psalms 23: 5; (21) Luke 11:3; (22) James 4:8; (23) James 1:5-7; (24) Hebrews 11:6; (25) 1 John 3:23; (26) Matthew 6:33; (27) Psalms 136:12; (28) Psalms 100:5; (29) Proverbs 3:5-6.

Bible Prayer: Precious Lord, you hear and answer my prayers.[1] This reality is too wonderful for me. As you supply the answers to each of my requests, faith and gratitude build in my heart.[2] I know that my effectual, fervent prayer will be heard and answered.[3] You always respond to a prayer of faith.[4] This knowledge gives me great joy and peace. You are my prayer-answering Father,[5] and I love you.[6] In Jesus' name,[7] Amen.

References: *(1) Psalms 91:15; (2) Philippians 4:6; (3) James 5:16; (4) Hebrews 11:6; (5) Matthew 21:22; (6) 1 John 4:20-21; (7) John 16:23.*

Related Scriptures: *1 Chronicles 5:20; 2 Chronicles 30:27; Ezra 8:23; Jonah 2:1; Matthew 21:22; Mark 1:35; Mark 11:24; John 15:7; Acts 4:31; Acts 6:6; Acts 10:31; 1 Peter 3:12; 1 John 5:15.*

44

MY PRAYERS PREVAIL

Bible Promise: "The effective, fervent prayer of a righteous man avails much" (James 5:16, NKJV).

Bible Meditation: Because God cares for me I do not have to worry about anything.[1] Through prayer, I can cast all my cares upon Him.[2] My loving Father knows what I need even before I pray, but He wants me to express my needs to Him.[3] In everything by prayer and supplication, with thanksgiving, I will let my requests be made to Him.[4] As a result, I will experience the peace of God that surpasses all understanding, and His peace will keep my heart and mind through Jesus Christ.[5]

God wants me to go before Him with confidence so that I will be able to obtain mercy and find grace to help in my time of need.[6] He wants me to express faith to Him so He will be able to reward me, and He wants me to seek Him diligently. In fact, without faith it is impossible to please Him.[7] The prayer of faith has the power to save the sick,[8] to open doors,[9] and to give me wisdom.[10] Therefore, I will pray the prayer of faith without wavering, and I will be single-minded as I trust in the Word of the Lord.[11]

With this in mind, I will have faith in God[12] when I pray. When I pray I will believe that I have received my petitions, because I know that God rewards this kind of faith.[13] I will pray in accordance with His will, as it is revealed in His Word, and as I do so, confidence and faith will build in my heart to appropriate all God has for me. I know that if I ask anything according to the will of God, He will hear me. Because I know He hears me when I pray, I know that He will grant the petitions I present to Him.[14] I will pray to the Father in the Name of Jesus so that He may give me my requests.[15]

With these truths in mind, I will continue instant in prayer while rejoicing in hope and being patient in tribulation.[16] I will rejoice evermore.[17] I will pray without ceasing.[18] In everything I will give thanks for I know this is God's will in Christ Jesus concerning me.[19] The Lord's eyes are watching me, and His ears are open to my prayers.[20] Evening, and morning, and at noon, I will pray and cry out to my God, knowing that He does indeed hear my voice.[21] I will pray always with all prayer and supplication in the Spirit, and I know the power of God will prevail in my life and in the lives of others for whom I pray.[22]

References: *(1) 1 Peter 5:7; (2) 1 Peter 5:7; (3) Matthew 6:8; (4) Philippians 4:6; (5) Philippians 4:7; (6) Hebrews 4:16; (7) Hebrews 11:6; (8) James*

5:15; (9) Luke 11:9; (10) James 1:6; (11) James 1:7-8;
(12) Mark 11:22; (13) Mark 11:24; (14) 1 John
5:14-15; (15) John 16:23; (16) Romans 12:12;
(17) 1 Thessalonians 5:16; (18) 1 Thessalonians
5:17; (19) 1 Thessalonians 5:18;(20) 1 Peter 3:12;
(21) Psalms 55:17; (22) Ephesians 6:18.

Bible Prayer: Loving Father,[1] as I pray to you
in the secret place you will reward me openly.[2]
Your name is holy.[3] Let your kingdom come in
my life, and let your will be done in and
through me.[4] Thank you for your promise to
give me my daily bread,[5] and to supply all my
needs according to your riches in glory.[6]
Forgive me of my sins as I forgive those who sin
against me.[7] I know you will not lead me into
temptation, but you will deliver me from evil,
for yours is the kingdom and the power
and the glory forever.[8] By walking in your
righteousness,[9] and praying according to your
will,[10] Lord, I know my prayers will be effective
and powerful.[11] In Jesus' name I pray,[12] Amen.

References: (1) Matthew 6:8; (2) Matthew 6:6;
(3) Matthew 6:9; (4) Matthew 6:10; (5) Matthew
6:11; (6) Philippians 4:19; (7) Matthew 6:12;
(8) Matthew 6:13; (9) 2 Timothy 2:22; (10) 1 John
5:14-15; (11) James 5:16; (12) John 16:24.

Related Scriptures: Psalms 5:2; Psalms 32:6;
Jeremiah 33:3; Matthew 18:18-19; 1 Corinthians
7:5; Ephesians 3:20; Colossians 4:2.

PRESENCE

45

GOD IS WITH ME

Bible Promise: "Let your conduct be without covetousness; be content with such things as you have. For He Himself has said, 'I will never leave you nor forsake you.'" (Heb. 13:5, NKJV).

Bible Meditation: God wants me to spend time with Him,[1] to develop an intimate relationship with Him,[2] because He loves me[3] and always wants the best for me.[4] He has promised never to leave me nor forsake me.[5] Jesus said that He will be with me always, even to the end of the age.[6]

The presence of God's Holy Spirit fills me with peace, love, and joy.[7] He is ever with me,[8] and I recognize my need for practicing His presence each step of my way.[9]

God is so good to me.[10] He is the One who is always there.[11] Truly, He answers when I call.[12] How I need Him in my life each moment of every day.[13]

The Father is my refuge,[14] my safe place,[15] my high tower,[16] my rock,[17] my strength,[18] my security.[19] In Him I live and move and have my being.[20] He is all in all to me.[21]

In Jesus Christ, my Lord, all things hold together.[22] He is the center of my life even as He is the center of world history.[23] How I love Him![24]

I choose, as Mary did, to engage in the most necessary responsibility of my life — to spend time with Jesus, sitting at His footstool, learning to know and to love Him.[25]

God goes with me throughout this day.[26] Nothing will happen today that He and I cannot handle together. His everlasting arms support me.[27] He leads the way for me.[28] He protects me[29] and empowers me.[30] I know I will never have to walk alone, for He always walks with me.[31] He holds my hand and lifts me up.[32] I now experience the fullness of joy I always find in His presence.[33]

References: (1) *John 14:3; (2) John 17:23; (3) 1 John 4:19; (4) Psalms 37:4; (5) Hebrews 13:5; (6) Matthew 28:20; (7) Galatians 5:22; (8) John 14:16-17; (9) Galatians 5:16; (10) Zechariah 9:17; (11) Psalms 46:1; (12) Jeremiah 33:3; (13) Hebrews 4:16; (14) Psalms 46:1; (15) Psalms 91:2; (16) Psalms 18:2; (17) Psalms 18:2; (18) Psalms 27:1; (19) Job 11:18; (20) Acts 17:28; (21) 1 Corinthians 12:6; (22) Colossians 1:17; (23) Colossians 1:27; (24) 1 John 4:19; (25) Luke 10:42; (26) Psalms 23:4; (27) Deuteronomy 33:27; (28) Psalms 23:2-3; (29) Deuteronomy 32:38; (30) Romans 15:13; (31) Psalms 140:13; (32) Psalms 3:3; (33) Psalms 16:11.*

Bible Prayer: Thank you, Father-God,[1] for your promise to remain with me.[2]   I enjoy your guiding presence in my life.[3]   Indeed, I feel enveloped by your presence and embraced by your loving arms.[4] I will walk in your presence throughout this day.[5] In Jesus' name[6] I receive your promise,[7] Amen.

References: (1) 2 Thessalonians 1:1; (2) Hebrews 13:5; (3) Psalms 100; (4) Psalms 89:21; (5) Psalms 23:4; (6) John 16:23; (7) John 16:24.

Related Scriptures: Deuteronomy 31:6; Psalms 16:11; Psalms 21:6; Psalms 31:20; Psalms 41:12; Hosea 6:2; Matthew 28:10; Acts 2:28.

46

EVERY PROMISE IN THE BOOK IS MINE

Bible Promise: "Blessed be the Lord, that hath given rest unto his people Israel, according to all that he promised: there hath not failed one word of all his good promise, which he promised by the hand of Moses his servant" (1 Kings 8:56).

Bible Meditation: God, my eternal Father,[1] established His covenant with Abraham[2] and the people of God.[2] My relationship with Him is based on His everlasting covenant[3] through the blood of Christ, my Lord.[4] He is the great Promise-keeper and not one word of His promises has ever failed.[5] To receive His promises I must stand in faith,[6] nothing wavering,[7] and trust Him with all my heart.[8]

The Lord remembers His promises.[9] He fulfills His promises.[10] The promise is to me and to all who believe.[11] I am a child of God's promise.[12] The Holy Spirit is the Spirit of God's promise.[13] All His promises are yes and amen in Christ Jesus.[14]

I am an heir of God's promises.[15] I have been sealed with the Holy Spirit of promise.[16] I am a partaker of God's promises in Christ by the gospel.[17] I know whom I have believed, and I am persuaded that he is able to keep that which I have committed unto Him[18] — my life, my health, my finances, my family, my future, my career, my marriage, and all things.

My confidence is in God.[19] I believe His Word which is a lamp unto my feet and a light unto my path.[20] I know that God is able to do exceedingly abundantly above all that I can ask or think.[21] In fact, all things are possible with Him.[22] He has promised me eternal life,[23] prosperity,[24] blessings,[25] victory,[26] forgiveness,[27] newness of life,[28] and so many other wonderful things. I believe God, that it shall be just as He has promised me in His Word.[29]

God will reward my faith in His promises.[30] Through patience[31] and perseverance,[32] if I do the will of God, I will receive His promises.[33] The Lord is not slack concerning His promise,[34] but He is patient and kind. God cannot lie.[35] He promised abundant life[36] and eternal life[37] to me before the world began.[38] He is the Promise-keeper and I am a promise-reaper.[39]

References: (1) Deuteronomy 33:27; (2) Genesis 17; (3) Genesis 17:7; (4) Hebrews 9:12; (5) 1 Kings 8:56; (6) Hebrews 11:6; (7) James 1:6; (8) Proverbs 3:5-6; (9) 2 Peter 3:9; (10) 2 Corinthians 7:1; (11) Acts 2:39; (12) Romans 9:8; (13) Ephesians 1:13; (14) 2 Corinthians 1:20; (15) Hebrews 11:9; (16) Ephesians 1:13; (17) Ephesians 3:6; (18) 2 Timothy 1:12; (19) Proverbs 3:26; (20) Psalms 119:105;

(21) Ephesians 3:20; (22) Matthew 19:26; (23) John 3:16; (24) Joshua 1:8; (25) Deuteronomy 28:2; (26) 1 Corinthians 15:57; (27) 1 John 1:9; (28) Romans 6:4; (29) Acts 27:25; (30) Hebrews 11:6; (31) Hebrews 6:12; (32) Ephesians 6:18; (33) Hebrews 10:36; (34) 2 Peter 3:9; (35) Titus 1:2; (36) John 10:10; (37) 1 John 5:13; (38) Ephesians 1:4; (39) Galatians 6:9.

Bible Prayer: Loving God, I thank you for the promises you have given to me.[1] I believe your Word.[2] I believe in you, and I know you will reward my belief.[3] There are thousands of promises in your Word and each one is for me. I know that all your promises are fulfilled in Jesus Christ, my Lord and Savior.[4] I receive your promises[5] with joy and thanksgiving. Your exceedingly great and precious promises are for me.[6] I rejoice,[7] dear Lord, as I obtain your promises.[8] How I praise you for making every promise mine! In Jesus' name[9] I pray, Amen.

References: *(1) 2 Corinthians 7:1; (2) Acts 4:4; (3) Hebrews 11:6; (4) 2 Corinthians 1:20; (5) Hebrews 11:17; (6) 2 Peter 1:4; (7) Philippians 4:4; (8) Hebrews 11:33; (9) John 15:16.*

Related Scriptures: *Psalms 105:42; Luke 24:49; Acts 2:33; Acts 26:6; Romans 4:20; Galatians 3:22; Hebrews 4:1; Hebrews 10;36; 1 John 2:25.*

47

GOD WANTS ME TO PROSPER

Bible Promise: "Beloved, I wish above all things that thou mayest prosper and be in health, even as thy soul prospereth" (3 John 2).

Bible Meditation: God wants me to prosper.[1] I will seek Him because I know He will not withhold any good thing from those who love Him.[2] I will seek first His kingdom and His righteousness, and I know everything I need will be provided for me.[3] My loving Father will supply all my needs according to His riches in glory by Christ Jesus.[4] He knows what I need even before I express it to Him.[5]

I have been young, and now I am older, and throughout my life I have never seen God forsake the righteous. I have never seen the children of the righteous having to go around begging for food.[6] Therefore, I will hearken to the voice of the Lord, my God, who promises that all His blessings will overtake me.[7] He will make me plenteous in goods and in health. He will open His treasure house to me and He will bless the work of my hands. I shall never have to borrow money again. He will make me the head, and not the tail. He will put me on the top, not on the bottom. These are His promises to me if I will obey His Word.[8] For the blessing of the Lord makes one rich, and He adds no sorrow with it.[9]

My Father takes pleasure in giving me the desires of my heart.[10] In fact, it is His good pleasure to give me His kingdom.[11] I will learn to give as He has given to me, and good measure, pressed down, and shaken together and running over will be my portion.[12] My Father in heaven will open the windows of His storehouse and pour out a blessing upon me that I shall not even be able to contain.[13] He will rebuke the devourer for my sake.[14]

I will not walk in the counsel of the ungodly nor stand in the way of sinners. Neither will I sit in the seat of the scornful. Rather, I will delight myself in the Word of God. I will meditate on the Scriptures day and night. This will make me like a tree that is planted by the river, a fruitful tree that will always prosper. Whatever I do shall prosper. This is because the Lord knows the way of the righteous, but the way of the ungodly shall perish.[15]

His Word shall not depart out of my mouth. I will meditate upon His precepts continually, and I will obey His Word. I want to live in accord with the Scriptures because I know this is the Father's will for me. He will reward me by making my way prosperous and giving me good success.[16] He owns the cattle on a thousand hills,[17] and He is able to do exceeding abundantly above all I can ask or think.[18]

References: *(1) Psalms 23:1; (2) Psalms 34:10; (3) Matthew 6:33; (4) Philippians 4:19; (5) Matthew 6:8; (6) Psalms 37:25; (7) Deuteronomy 28:2; (8) Deuteronomy 28:11-13; (9) Proverbs 10:22; (10) Psalms 37:4; (11) Luke 12:32; (12) Luke 6:38; (13) Malachi 3:10; (14) Malachi 3:11; (15) Psalms 1; (16) Joshua 1:8; (17) Psalms 50:10; (18) Ephesians 3:20.*

Bible Prayer: Heavenly Father,[1] you know all my needs.[2] You have promised to supply all my needs according to your riches in glory by Christ Jesus.[3] I thank you and praise you for your great faithfulness to me.[4] You desire that I prosper in all things and be in health, even as my soul prospers.[5]

You are bringing me into a good land where there are brooks of water, flowing fountains and abounding springs. It is a land of wheat, barley, vines, fig trees, pomegranates, olive oil, and honey. It is a place of abundance where there is plentiful bread to eat and there is no lack of any good thing. The stones in this land are iron and there is brass in its hills. Jehovah-jireh, my provider, thank you for prospering me in this rich land you have provided for me. I can eat to the full and there is still plenty left over.

For all these reasons I praise and bless your name, O Lord. I will never forget you. I will keep your commandments, your judgments, and your statutes. Thank you for the promise that you will multiply my herds and flocks. You will increase my silver and gold. All that I own will be multiplied.

My heart is lifted up by your graciousness to me. You brought me out of captivity in the land of Egypt and brought me into the land of promise. It is you, the Lord, my God, who gives me the power to be wealthy because this is a part of your eternal covenant with me and with all who call upon you.[6]

I will bless you at all times. Your praise shall continually be in my mouth.[7] My soul will make its boast in you.[8] I will magnify you and exalt your name.[9] Your lovingkindness is better than life to me.[10] In Jesus' name I pray,[11] Amen.

References: (1) Matthew 6:32; (2) Matthew 6:32; (3) Philippians 4:19; (4) Lamentations 3:23; (5) 3 John 2; (6) Deuteronomy 8:7-14, 18; (7) Psalms 34:1; (8) Psalms 34:2; (9) Psalms 34:3; (10) Psalms 63:3; (11) John 16:24.

Related Scriptures: Deuteronomy 28:4-8; 1 Corinthians 16:2; Matthew 10:8; 2 Corinthians 9:6-8.

48

GOD PROTECTS ME

Bible Promise: "Fear not, for I have redeemed you; I have called you by your name; you are Mine. When you pass through the waters, I will be with you; And through the rivers, they shall not overflow you. When you walk through the fire, you shall not be burned, Nor shall the flame scorch you. For I am the Lord your God, the Holy One of Israel, your Savior" (Isa. 43:1-3, NKJV).

Bible Meditation: The Lord is my shield. He is my glory and the lifter of my head.[1] He is my refuge and strength — a very present help in time of trouble.[2] I put my trust in Him because He is my protection.[3] He is my rock and my fortress and my deliverer. God is my strength and I will always trust in Him. He is my buckler and He is the horn of my salvation. He is my high tower.[4]

He is showing me His ways and teaching me His paths.[5] His eyes run to and fro, throughout the whole earth, and He shows himself strong in my behalf because my heart is loyal and pure before Him.[6] I will sing of His power and of His mercy because He is my defense — my protection — and He is my refuge.[7] He will fight for me.[8] He only is my rock and my salvation. He is my defense. I shall not be moved.[9] He is my hope and my trust.[10]

The Lord is faithful to me. He will establish me and He will guard me from the evil one.[11] I will sing of His mercies forever. With my mouth I will make known His salvation to all generations.[12] The eternal God is my refuge, and underneath me are His everlasting arms. He will thrust out the enemy from before me.[13] For the Lord will go before me, and the God of Israel will be my rear guard.[14]

I will lift up my eyes unto the Lord for He is my protector and my helper. He will not permit my foot to be moved. He keeps me in His love. He never slumbers nor sleeps. The Lord is my Keeper, and He will preserve me from all evil. He will preserve my soul. The Lord preserves my going out and my coming in forevermore.[15] The Lord is in the midst of His people. He is the Mighty One who saves me and He will rejoice over me with joy. I will rest in His love for me. He will rejoice over me with singing.[16]

When the enemy shall come in like a flood, the Spirit of the Lord will raise a standard against him.[17] God's power is truly awesome. The greatness of His power causes His enemies to submit themselves to Him.[18] All the earth shall worship Him and sing unto Him.[19] He rules by His power forever.[20]

God hears me when I cry unto Him. He attends to the voice of my prayer.[21] Blessed be the name of the Lord.[22]

References: (1) Psalms 3:3; (2) Psalms 46:1; (3) Psalms 7:1; (4) Psalms 18:2; (5) Psalms 25:4; (6) 2 Chronicles 16:9; (7) Psalms 59:16; (8) Deuteronomy 1:30; (9) Psalms 62:6; (10) Psalms 71:5; (11) 2 Thessalonians 3:3; (12) Psalms 89:1; (13) Deuteronomy 33:27; (14) Isaiah 52:12; (15) Psalms 121; (16) Zephaniah 3:17; (17) Isaiah 59:19; (18) Psalms 66:3; (19) Psalms 66:4; (20) Psalms 66:7; (21) Psalms 66:19; (22) Psalms 144:1.

Bible Prayer: Lord God,[1] you have always been a shelter and a protection for me. You are my strong tower, my defense against the enemy.[2] You have promised to keep me.[3] Thank you, Lord. I place all my trust in you. Let me never be in confusion.[4] I know, Father, that you are not the author of confusion.[5] You are the God of all peace.[6] I know you will always deliver me in your righteousness and enable me to escape.[7] You are faithful to me and you will never permit me to be tempted above my ability to be able to bear it. You always provide a way of escape for me.[8] You are my strong habitation, Lord, and you are my rock and my fortress.[9] My mouth will be filled with your praises and with your honor every day,[10] because I know you will never be far from me.[11] You, O Lord, are my protection.[12] In Jesus' name I pray,[13] Amen.

References: *(1) Exodus 3:18; (2) Psalms 61:3; (3) 1 Samuel 2:9; (4) Psalms 71:1; (5) 1 Corinthians 14:33; (6) Hebrews 13:20; (7) Psalms 71:2; (8) 1 Corinthians 10:13; (9) Psalms 71:3; (10) Psalms 71:8; (11) Psalms 71:12; (12) Psalms 46:1; (13) John 16:23.*

Related Scriptures: *Deuteronomy 1:30; Job 22:25; Psalms 59:9; Psalms 59:16-17; Psalms 62:2; Psalms 62:6; Psalms 89:18; Psalms 94:22.*

RELATIONSHIP

49

I AM GOD'S CHILD

Bible Promise: "But as many as received him, to them gave he power to become the sons of God, even to them that believe on his name: Which were born, not of blood, nor of the will of the flesh, nor of the will of man, but of God" (John 1:12-13).

Bible Meditation: I am a child of God[1] who has been adopted[2] by my heavenly Father[3] into the family of God. All believers are my brothers and sisters in Christ.[4] My Father in heaven loves me.[5] He wants to meet my needs.[6] He cares about every aspect of my life.[7] God loves me with an everlasting love.[8]

It is my Father's good pleasure to give me His kingdom[9] which does not consist of meat and drink, but of righteousness, peace, and joy in His Holy Spirit.[10] I love my Father, and when I reflect on His great love for me,[11] my heart is filled with gratitude and I cry, "Abba [Papa], Father."[12]

Through prayer[13] and worship[14] I have a personal and intimate relationship with my Father. As Jesus prayed, I desire to be one with Him,[15] with Jesus Christ, my Lord,[16] and with my brothers and sisters.[17] My heavenly Father is my safe place, my refuge,[18] my high tower,[19] my Rock,[20] my Guide,[21] my Defender,[22] and my friend.[23]

My Father knows what I need before I ask Him.[24] He wants to give me the desires of my heart.[25] He supplies all my needs according to His riches in glory.[26] I dwell in the secret place of my Father — the most-high God.[27] I will abide under His shadow.[28] I will declare to others that He is my Fortress, and I will trust in Him.[29] He will deliver me from Satan's snares, including sickness.[30] He will cover me with His feathers, and His truth will be my shield and buckler.[31] I will not be afraid of any terror or harm.[32] He will give His angels charge over me, and they will keep me in all my ways.[33] When I call upon Him, He will answer me.[34] He will be with me in times of trouble.[35] He will give me long life.[36]

My heavenly Father has given me eternal life, and this life is in His Son, my Lord and Savior, Jesus Christ.[37] The Word of God declares to me that I have eternal life, and that I can know beyond all doubt that everlasting life is mine.[38] I believe on the Name of Jesus Christ and because I do, I know I will live forever.[39]

References: *(1) John 1:12; (2) Galatians 4:5; (3) Luke 11:2; (4) 1 Corinthians 12:27; (5) John 3:16;*

(6) Philippians 4:19; (7) Matthew 6:30; (8) Psalms 136:1; (9) Luke 12:32; (10) Romans 14:17; (11) Romans 5:8; (12) Mark 14:36; (13) Ephesians 6:18; (14) Psalms 29:2; (15) John 17:21; (16) John 17:23; (17) John 17:21; (18) Psalms 46:1; (19) Psalms 18:2; (20) Psalms 18:2; (21) Psalms 48:14; (22) Psalms 59:1; (23) John 15:15; (24) Matthew 6:8; (25) Psalms 37:4; (26) Philippians 4:19; (27) Psalms 91:1; (28) Psalms 91:1; (29) Psalms 91:2; (30) Psalms 91:3; (31) Psalms 91:4; (32) Psalms 91:5; (33) Psalms 91:11; (34) Psalms 91:15; (35) Psalms 91:15; (36) Psalms 91:16; (37) 1 John 5:13; (38) 1 John 5:11; (39) 1 John 5:10.

Bible Prayer: Heavenly Father,[1] it is so good to be your child.[2] You lead me,[3] guide me,[4] correct me,[5] teach me,[6] love me,[7] provide for me,[8] nurture me,[9] speak to me,[10] hold my hand,[11] shelter me,[12] defend me,[13] and keep me.[14] I love you, Father.[15] Thank you for accepting me,[16] restoring me,[17] redeeming me,[18] and supporting me.[19] I will worship[20] and adore you[21] forever.[22]

References: *(1) Isaiah 9:6; (2) Galatians 3:26; (3) Psalms 23:2; (4) Psalms 73:24; (5) Psalms 94:12; (6) Psalms 27:11; (7) Psalms 36:7; (8) Philippians 1:19; (9) Ephesians 6:4; (10) Isaiah 45:19; (11) Psalms 94:18; (12) Psalms 61:3; (13) Psalms 94:22; (14) Isaiah 26:3; (15) 1 John 4:19; (16) Ephesians 1:6; (17) Joel 2:25; (18) Hosea 13:14; (19) Deuteronomy 33:27; (20) Psalms 96:9; (21) Revelation 4:10; (22) Psalms 100.*

Related Scriptures: *Matthew 5:9; Luke 20:36; Romans 8:16; Romans 8:17; Romans 8:21; Romans 9:26; Galatians 3:26; 1 John 3:10.*

RESTORATION

50

GOD RESTORES ME WHEN I FALL

Bible Promise: "He who conceals his sins does not prosper, but whoever confesses and renounces them finds mercy. Blessed is the man who always fears the Lord, but he who hardens his heart falls into trouble" (Prov. 28:13-14, NIV).

Bible Meditation: God gives me power when I am faint, and when I feel weak He increases my strength.[1] When I wait upon Him, He renews my strength and enables me to mount up with wings as an eagle. His power enables me to run and not be weary, to walk and not faint.[2] I will keep His Word because He is good and He is teaching me His statutes.[3] I will trust Him with all my heart. In all my ways I will acknowledge Him, and I know He will direct my paths.[4]

I will make straight paths for my feet[5] and follow peace with all men, and holiness, without which I shall not be able to see the Lord.[6] By striving for purity of heart at all times I know I will see the Lord.[7] I thank you that you will never cast me aside, and you will never forsake your inheritance.[8] Whoever comes to Christ will in no wise be cast out.[9]

God is my Father and He loves me freely. When I slide back He heals me.[10] When I confess my sins to Him He is faithful and just to forgive me of my sins and to cleanse me from all unrighteousness.[11] He brings my soul out of prison so that I will praise His name. He always deals bountifully with me.[12]

God's mercy is everlasting. Therefore, I will give thanks to Him.[13] He alone does great wonders.[14] God promises to restore to me what the devil has taken from me, and His plentiful provision will see me through every crisis.[15] He is the Lord, my God, and I know I shall never be ashamed because He is always there for me.[16] When I am brought low, He lifts me up. He delivers me from my persecutors.[17]

The goodness of God leads me to repentance,[18] as godly sorrow for the wrongs I've done rises up within me.[19] Worldly sorrow leads to death, but godly sorrow leads to the kind of repentance that restores me to a right relationship with my Father in heaven.[20] I confess my sins to the Father now: _____ _____, and as I do so I know He has restored me to fellowship.[21]

Because I have repented and confessed my sins I know that my sins have been blotted out. This is the promise of my Father. Even now I am experiencing the times of refreshing that He sends to me from His presence.[22]

References: *(1) Isaiah 40:29; (2) Isaiah 40:31; (3) Psalms 119:67-68; (4) Proverb 3:5-6; (5) Hebrews 12:13; (6) Hebrews 12:14; (7) Matthew 5:8; (8) Psalms 94:14; (9) John 6:37; (10) Hosea 14:4; (11) 1 John 1:9; (12) Psalms 142:7; (13) Psalms 136:1; (14) Psalms 136:4; (15) Joel 2:25-26; (16) Joel 2:26-27; (17) Psalms 142:7; (18) Romans 2:4; (19) 2 Corinthians 7:10; (20) 2 Corinthians 7:10; (21) 1 John 1:3; (22) Acts 3:19.*

Bible Prayer: Lord God,[1] thank you for the promise of restoration.[2] Thank you for granting repentance to me,[3] for forgiving my sins, and cleansing me from all unrighteousness.[4] There is, therefore, now no condemnation to me, and I choose to walk in your Spirit rather than after the flesh.[5] I now realize that to be spiritually minded is life and peace, but to be carnally minded is death.[6] As you remove the dross from my life, I know a vessel for the finer shall come forth.[7] Speaking the truth in love, Father, I will grow up in all things. In the name of Jesus I pray,[8] Amen.

References: *(1) Ezekiel 39:29; (2) Jeremiah 30:17; (3) 2 Timothy 2:25; (4) 1 John 1:19; (5) Romans 8:1; (6) Romans 8:6; (7) Proverbs 25:4; (8) John 15:16.*

Related Scriptures: *Psalms 51:12; Matthew 17:11.*

51

REVIVAL IS COMING!

Bible Promise: "Arise, shine; for your light has come! And the glory of the Lord is risen upon you. For behold, darkness shall cover the earth, and deep darkness the people; But the Lord will arise over you, and His glory will be seen upon you. The Gentiles shall come to your light, and kings to the brightness of your rising" (Isa. 60:1-2, NKJV).

Bible Meditation: The Lord is never slack regarding His promises, because He is not willing that anyone should perish. He wants everyone to come to repentance.[1] His Word will never return unto Him void, but it will always accomplish His purposes.[2] This truth enables me to go out with joy and to be led forth with peace.[3] I will be patient, therefore, unto the coming of the Lord because I know the early and latter rain will come.[4]

God will pour out His Spirit upon all flesh. Sons and daughters will prophesy. Old men will dream dreams. Young men will see visions. There will be wonders in the heavens and on the earth. The sun shall be turned into darkness, and the moon will be turned red before the great and the terrible Day of the Lord arrives. When all this happens, whoever shall call on the name of the Lord will be delivered.[5] The earth will be filled with the knowledge of the glory of the Lord as the waters cover the sea.[6]

God will do a new thing in our midst. He will make a way in the wilderness and rivers in the desert.[7] Every valley will be exalted and every mountain and hill will be lowered. The crooked places will be made straight and the rough places will be made smooth. The glory of the Lord will be revealed, and all flesh will see it because God's Word has spoken this.[8] As the earth brings forth the buds of springtime and the gardens spring forth with new life, the Lord God will cause righteousness and praise to spring forth before all the nations.[9]

During the time of revival that will soon come upon us, God will seek that which was lost and bring again that which was driven away. He will bind up that which was broken and strengthen that which was sick. His judgment will prevail.[10]

The Gospel of the Kingdom will be preached in all the world for a witness unto all nations.[11] Heaven and earth will pass away but the Word of the Lord will abide forever.[12] I will remember His words. I will prepare for the coming revival through intercessory prayer,[13] studying the Word of God,[14] building myself up in the faith,[15] keeping myself in the love of God,[16] looking for the mercy of the Lord Jesus Christ,[17] and preaching the Gospel of Jesus Christ wherever I go.[18]

References: (1) 2 Peter 3:9; (2) Isaiah 55:11; (3) Isaiah 55:12; (4) James 5:7; (5) Joel 2:28-32; (6) Habakkuk 2:14; (7) Isaiah 43:19; (8) Isaiah 40:3-5; (9) Isaiah 61:11; (10) Ezekiel 34:16; (11) Matthew 24:14; (12) Matthew 24:35; (13) Ezekiel 22:30; (14) 2 Timothy 2:15; (15) Jude 20; (16) Jude 21; (17) Jude 21; (18) Matthew 28:19-20.

Bible Prayer: O Lord,[1] I thank you for your promise of revival.[2] Hasten the day, Father, when the ends of the world shall remember and turn back to you, and the people of all the nations will worship you.[3] The kingdoms of the world are yours, Lord; and you are the governor of the nations.[4] The king's heart is in your hand, and like the rivers of water, you turn it in whatever direction you choose.[5] Turn the hearts of our leaders and people back to you, Father.

You have promised that we shall be able to rebuild the old wastes and raise up the former desolations. Through faith in you we shall be able to repair the cities, the desolation of many generations.[6] Reveal your glory, Lord.[7] Speak your gracious invitation to the hearts of people everywhere, inviting them to come to you and to take of the water of life freely.[8] Assure people, Lord, that if they will come to you, you will in no wise cast them out.[9]

Lord, bare your holy arm before the eyes of all nations so that all the nations of the earth will see your salvation. May people everywhere consider your gospel which they may not have heard before.[10] May there be no speech or language where your gospel is not preached. Let your prevailing Word reach to the end of the world. Let your people, Father, be your tabernacle which, as a bridegroom coming out of his chamber, rejoices as a strong man to run a race.[11]

Reveal to people, Lord, that all flesh is as grass and all the glory of man is as the flower of grass. The grass withers and the flowers of grass fall away, but your Word endures forever.[12] In Jesus' name I pray,[13] Amen.

References: *(1) Leviticus 1:1; (2) Joel 2:28-32; (3) Psalms 22:27; (4) Psalms 22:28; (5) Proverbs 21:1; (6) Isaiah 61:4; (7) Isaiah 40:5; (8) Revelation 22:17; (9) John 6:37; (10) Isaiah 52:10; (11) Psalms 19:3-5; (12) 1 Peter 1:24-25; (13) John 16:24.*

Related Scriptures: *Habakkuk 2:3; Matthew 24:14; Matthew 24:44; Acts 2:17-21; 1 Timothy 4:1-3; 2 Timothy 4:3-4; 2 Peter 3:10.*

52

THE JOY OF THE LORD IS MY STRENGTH

Bible Promise: "This day is holy to our Lord. Do not sorrow, for the joy of the Lord is your strength" (Neh. 8:10, NKJV).

Bible Meditation: God's Word brings me joy — a full joy that remains within me.[1] God has not given me a spirit of fear, but one of power and love and a sound mind.[2] This fact makes me rejoice in the Lord.[3]

This is the day that the Lord has made. I will rejoice and be glad in it.[4] Because I have placed my unswerving trust in the Lord, I will rejoice. I will even shout for joy because He is my Protector. I will love His name and be joyful in Him because I know He will bless me; His loving favor will surround me like a shield.[5]

A merry heart does me good like a medicine. It improves my health.[6] It gives me a happy countenance.[7] God restores the joy of His salvation to me. He upholds me, and this causes me to reach out to others.[8] My Father has anointed me with the oil of gladness because I love righteousness and hate wickedness.[9]

In the presence of the Lord there is fullness of joy.[10] As I go before Him, my heart is filled with joy because He is my joy.[11] I will praise Him and hope in Him because He is the health of my countenance.[12] Behold, God is my salvation. I will trust Him and not be afraid: for the Lord Jehovah is my strength and my song. Therefore, with joy I will draw water from His wells of salvation. Today I praise Him and call upon His name. I will declare His works among the people and exalt His name. I will sing unto Him with joy for He has done excellent things.[13] I will ask and I receive that my joy may be full.[14] God fills me with joy and peace when I believe His Word.[15]

Knowing God and His salvation fills me with joy unspeakable and full of glory.[16] This day is holy unto the Lord. Therefore, I will not be sad nor sorry, because I know the joy of the Lord is my strength.[17]

References: *(1) John 15:11; (2) 2 Timothy 1:7; (3) 1 Thessalonians 5:16; (4) Psalms 118:24; (5) Psalms 5:11-12; (6) Proverbs 17:22; (7) Proverbs 15:13; (8) Psalms 51:12-13; (9) Psalms 45:7-8; (10) Psalms 16:11; (11) Psalms 43:4; (12) Psalms 43:5; (13) Isaiah 12:2-5; (14) John 16:24; (15) Romans 15:13; (16) 1 Peter 1:8; (17) Nehemiah 8:10.*

Bible Prayer: Heavenly Father,[1] thank you for the fruit of joy in my life.[2] Thank you for preserving me. I place all my trust in you.[3] I will always set you before me. Because you are at my right hand, I know I shall not be moved.[4] Therefore, my heart is glad and my glory rejoices. My flesh also rests in hope.[5] You are showing me the path of life.

In your presence there is fullness of joy. At your right hand there are pleasures forevermore.[6] I will always love you, O Lord, because you are my strength.[7] The joy you impart to me is my strength.[8] You are my rock and my fortress. You are my Deliverer, my God, my strength, my buckler, the horn of my salvation, and my high tower.[9]

I will call upon you because you are worthy to be praised; and as I do so, I know you will save me from all my enemies.[10] I receive the promises of your Word with the joy of the Holy Spirit.[11] In Jesus' name I pray,[12] Amen.

References: *(1) Matthew 26:39; (2) Galatians 5:22; (3) Psalms 16:1; (4) Psalms 16:8; (5) Psalms 16:9; (6) Psalms 16:11; (7) Psalms 18:1; (8) Nehemiah 8:10; (9) Psalms 18:2; (10) Psalms 18:3; (11) 1 Thessalonians 1:6; (12) John 16:23.*

Related Scriptures: *Jeremiah 31:13; Matthew 25:21,23; Acts 13:52; Romans 5:11; Philemon 7; 1 John 1:4.*

STRENGTH

53

WHEN I AM WEAK, THEN I AM STRONG

Bible Promise: "'My grace is sufficient for you, for My strength is made perfect in weakness.' Therefore most gladly I will rather boast in my infirmities, that the power of Christ may rest upon me. Therefore I take pleasure in infirmities, in reproaches, in needs, in persecutions, in distresses, for Christ's sake. For when I am weak, then I am strong" (2 Cor. 12:9-10, NKJV).

Bible Meditation: Without Christ I can do nothing,[1] but through Him I can do all things because He strengthens me.[2] God girds me with strength when I am weak, and He makes my way perfect.[3] He makes my feet like hinds' feet and sets me upon high places.[4] He teaches my hands to war so that I can break a steel bow in my arms.[5]

He is the God of my strength.[6] He is my refuge and strength; He is a very present help in time of trouble.[7] When my strength fails and I am weak, He will not forsake me.[8] The Lord is my source of strength. He is my refuge in the storm, my shadow from the heat.[9] When I feel weak, I will say I am strong.[10]

I will wait on the Lord, and He will strengthen my heart.[11] I will be of good courage and I know He will strengthen my heart because all my hope is in Him.[12] He strengthens me according to the promises of His Word.[13] I will not fear for God is with me. I will not be dismayed because I know He is my God. He will strengthen me when I am weak. He will help me in my time of need. He will uphold me with the right hand of His righteousness.[14]

The God of all grace, who has called me unto His eternal glory by Christ Jesus, will make me whole. He will establish, strengthen, and settle me.[15] He is granting to me, according to His riches in glory, all the strength I need. He is indeed strengthening me with might by His Spirit in my inner being.[16]

The Lord is strengthening me with all might, according to His glorious power, unto all patience and longsuffering with joyfulness.[17] This makes me very thankful to the Father who has permitted me to be a partaker of the inheritance of the saints in light.[18] He has delivered me from the power and dominion of darkness and translated me into the Kingdom of the Son of His love.[19]

Whenever I feel weak, God will be the strength of my heart.[20]

References: (1) John 15:5; (2) Philippians 4:13;
(3) Psalms 18:32; (4) Psalms 18:33; (5) Psalms 18:34;
(6) Psalms 43:2; (7) Psalms 46:1; (8) Psalms 71:9;
(9) Isaiah 25:4; (10) Joel 3:10; (11) Psalms 27:14;
(12) Psalms 31:24; (13) Psalms 119:28; (14) Isaiah
41:10; (15) 1 Peter 5:10; (16) Ephesians 3:16;
(17) Colossians 1:11; (18) Colossians 1:12;
(19) Colossians 1:13; (20) Psalms 73:26.

Bible Prayer: Lord,[1] you are my lamp. You always lighten my darkness.[2] Through your strength I am able to run through a troop and leap over a wall.[3] Your way is perfect, Father. Your Word is proven. You are a buckler to all who trust in you.[4] I trust in you,[5] and in your Word.[6]

You are my rock.[7] You are my strength and power, and you make my way perfect.[8] Thank you, Father, for the shield of your salvation. Your gentleness has made me great.[9] You have enlarged my steps under me so that my feet will not slip.[10] You have girded me with strength for every battle.[11] You are the living Lord, my rock. Blessed be your name. I exalt you as the God of my salvation.[12] You are my avenger, Lord;[13] therefore, I will give thanks unto you and sing praises to your name.[14] You are the tower of my salvation,[15] and I love you.[16] In Jesus' name I pray,[17] Amen.

References: (1) Exodus 15:2; (2) 2 Samuel
22:29; (3) 2 Samuel 22:30; (4) 2 Samuel 22:31;

(5) Proverbs 3:5-6; (6) Psalms 119:42; (7) 2 Samuel 22:32; (8) 2 Samuel 22:33; (9) 2 Samuel 22:36; (10) 2 Samuel 22:37; (11) 2 Samuel 22:40; (12) 2 Samuel 22:47; (13) 2 Samuel 22:48; (14) 2 Samuel 22:50; (15) 2 Samuel 22:51; (16) 1 John 4:19; (17) John 16:23.

Related Scriptures: *Psalms 18:2; Psalms 19:14; Psalms 27:1; Psalms 29:11; Proverbs 10:29; Jeremiah 16:19; Romans 5:6.*

SUPPLY

54

ALL MY NEEDS WILL BE SUPPLIED

Bible Promise: "And my God shall supply all your need according to His riches in glory by Christ Jesus." (Phil. 4:19, NKJV).

Bible Meditation: My God is Jehovah-jireh, my provider.[1] He knows what I need, when I need it, and how best my needs can be met.[2] He delights in giving me the desires of my heart because He loves me and I love Him.[3]

The Lord's great mercies are new in my life each morning.[4] His grace and loving favor are upon me and within me.[5] His lovingkindness to me is better than life itself.[6] He will give me my daily bread,[7] and so much more, because He is the God of more than enough.[8]

My Father cares about me and my loved ones.[9] He wants our needs to be met. He does not fail; in fact, He cannot fail.[10] He fulfills all His promises in my life.[11]

God's Word will never return unto Him void.[12] His Word is for me. He expects me to stand upon the promises of His Word.[13] I take that stand, and through faith, I will never be moved.[14] God's Word fulfills what He says it will accomplish in my life. All His promises are yes and amen in Christ Jesus, my Lord.[15]

My Father is good to me.[16] He takes care of me and protects me.[17] He feeds the birds of the air, He clothes the lilies of the field, and He supplies all my needs.[18] He is the Creator of the universe and yet He knows all about me.[19] My God always does exceedingly abundantly beyond all I can ever ask or think.[20]

The Lord provides food for those who fear Him.[21] He gives clothing to the naked.[22] He is the ultimate Father who protects, provides for, and nourishes His children.[23] His protection, provision, and nurturing have been given to me to enjoy. I receive His blessings in my life this day.

God's provision in my life is super-abundant. All I have ever needed, need now, and will ever need His hands will supply.[24]

References: *(1) Matthew 6:33; (2) Matthew 6:8; (3) Psalms 37:4; (4) Lamentations 3:23; (5) 1 Thessalonians 5:28; (6) Psalms 63:3; (7) Luke 11:3; (8) Ephesians 3:20; (9) 1 Peter 5:7; (10) Matthew 19:26; (11) 2 Corinthians 1:20; (12) Isaiah 55:11; (13) 2 Peter 1:4; (14) Hebrews 6:12; (15) 2 Corinthians 1:20; (16) Psalms 25:8; (17) Deuteronomy 32:38; (18) Matthew 6:28-29; (19) Matthew 6:26; (20) Ephesians 3:20; (21) Psalms 146:7; (22) Matthew 6:30; (23) James 1:17; (24) Philippians 4:19.*

Bible Prayer: Great is your faithfulness, O God, my Father. Morning by morning new mercies I see.[1] All I need your hands will provide.[2] Thank you, Father, for your loving care and supply in my life.[3] I claim your promise today.[4] I believe it,[5] and I look forward to all you are going to do.[6] In Jesus' name I pray,[7] Amen.

References: (1) Lamentations 3:23; (2) Philippians 4:19; (3) Psalms 25:6; (4) Hebrews 6:12; (5) Hebrews 11:6; (6) Philippians 1:6; (7) John 15:16.

Related Scriptures: Genesis 22:14; Psalms 68:10; Psalms 111:5; Matthew 6:1; 1 Timothy 6:17.

55

I AM MORE THAN A CONQUEROR

Bible Promise: "Yet in all these things we are more than conquerors through Him who loved us" (Rom. 8:37, NKJV).

Bible Meditation: The Lord has promised me that all things work together for good in my life.[1] He also assures me that nothing — past, present, or future — will be able to separate me from His love.[2] There is absolutely nothing to worry about.[3]

When I am tried I can be sure that I will receive the crown of life because I love the Lord and this is His direct promise to me.[4] For this reason I can count it all joy when I fall into diverse temptations because I know that the trying of my faith will work patience into me.[5] When troubles come I can be sure that there is no suffering that can compare with the glory God will reveal to me.[6]

Being absolutely certain of these truths, therefore, I put on the whole armor of God.[7] His armor will enable me to withstand in the evil day, and I always want to stand upon the promises of God.[8] I gird my loins with His truth

and put on the breastplate of His righteousness.[9]
I place the preparation of the gospel of peace
upon my feet.[10]   I protect myself with the
shield of faith which enables me to quench all
the fiery darts of the wicked one.[11] My faith is
in the promises of God.[12] I wear the helmet of
salvation and my weapon is the sword of the
Spirit which is the Word of God.[13] His Word is
quick and powerful. It is a living Word, and it
is sharper than any two-edged sword; therefore,
it is my most effective weapon. It is able to
penetrate so deeply that it divides soul and
spirit and it is a discerner of the thoughts and
intents of my heart.[14]

I will always pray with all prayer and
supplication in the Spirit, and I will watch
thereunto with all perseverance and supplication
for all saints because I know the power of prayer
prevails in receiving all the promises of God.[15]
Nothing is too hard for my God.[16]

I put my trust in God who will never let
me grow confused.[17] He is not the author of
confusion.[18]   He will deliver me from all
trouble in His righteousness.[19] He is my strong
habitation, my rock, and my fortress.[20] God is
my hope.[21] In all things I will go forward in the
strength of the Lord, my God.[22] I will hope in
Him continually, and I will praise Him at all
times.[23] He inhabits my praises.[24]

Even in the face of troubles my God will impart life to me.[25] His righteousness and His greatness are beyond measure.[26] He will strengthen me and comfort me.[27] God is my Deliverer.[28] God is my defense.[29] God is my strength.[30] My heart is fixed on Him.[31] He is my glory and the lifter of my head.[32] Therefore, in all things, I am more than a conqueror through Him who loves me.[33]

References: (1) Romans 8:28; (2) Romans 8:38-39; (3) 1 Peter 5:7; (4) James 1:12; (5) James 1:2-3; (6) Romans 8:18; (7) Ephesians 6:11; (8) Ephesians 6:13; (9) Ephesians 6:14; (10) Ephesians 6:15; (11) Ephesians 6:16; (12) Hebrews 11:6; (13) Ephesians 6:17; (14) Hebrews 4:12; (15) Jeremiah 33:3; (16) Genesis 18:14; (17) Psalms 71:1; (18) 1 Corinthians 14:33; (19) Psalms 71:2; (20) Psalms 71:3; (21) Psalms 71:5; (22) Psalms 71:16; (23) Psalms 71:14; (24) Psalms 22:3; (25) Psalms 71:20; (26) Psalms 71:19; (27) Psalms 71:21; (28) Psalms 59:1; (29) Psalms 59:17; (30) Psalms 59:17; (31) Psalms 57:7; (32) Psalms 3:3; (33) Romans 8:37.

Bible Prayer: Heavenly Father,[1] you are so good to me.[2] You have promised to give me overcoming power[3] even when difficulties arise. I praise you and glorify you because you are great and greatly to be praised.[4] When the enemy comes in like a flood, Father, you will always raise a standard against him.[5] I have

the support of your everlasting arms beneath
me.[6] Your Word will keep me from sin.[7] I will
be victorious through faith in the Name of
Jesus Christ and His Word.[8] I praise you, Lord,
for the certain knowledge that all things will
work together for good for me because I have
been called according to your purpose.[9] In
Jesus' name[10] I pray, Amen.

References: *(1) Ephesians 1:2; (2) Psalms 106:1;
(3) 1 John 5:4; (4) Psalms 48:1; (5) Isaiah 59:19;
(6) Deuteronomy 33:27; (7) Psalms 119:11; (8) John
15:16; (9) Romans 8:28; (10) John 15:16.*

Related Scriptures: *Nahum 1:7; 2 Corinthians
4:8-9; Psalms 138:7; Isaiah 43:2; Psalms 121:1-2;
Philippians 4:6-7.*

56

NO WEAPON FORMED AGAINST ME WILL PROSPER

Bible Promise: "No weapon formed against you shall prosper; And every tongue which rises against you in judgment You shall condemn. This is the heritage of the servants of the Lord, And their righteousness is from Me" (Isa. 54:17, NKJV).

Bible Meditation: I have been set free from all condemnation.[1] Because this is true I am able to remain happy when others hate me, ostracize me, reproach me, and say evil things about me for Jesus' sake. I can even rejoice in that day and leap for joy, knowing that my reward will be great in heaven.[2]

I will love my enemies, bless them that curse me, do good to them that hate me, and pray for them that despitefully use me and persecute me because I am a child of my Father in heaven. He makes His sun to rise on the evil and on the good, and He sends rain on the just and on the unjust.[3] When I find myself suffering for righteousness' sake I will endeavor to remain happy. I will not be afraid or troubled. Instead,

I will sanctify the Lord God in my heart and I will prepare myself to always give an answer to everyone who asks me about the hope I have. In this way my persecutors may be ashamed for accusing me of wrong when I am trying to maintain a Christian life-style.[4]

The Lord is my defense; therefore, I do not have to defend myself. He is the rock of my refuge.[5] It is thankworthy when I suffer wrongfully and suffer for my walk with God. When I do well and still have to suffer for it, I will take it patiently, realizing that this is acceptable with God. Actually He called me to this because Christ suffered for me and left me an example so that I might be able to follow in His steps. He did not sin and no guile was found in His mouth. When He was reviled, He did not respond in kind. When he suffered, He did not complain.[6] I want to be like my Lord and Savior, Jesus Christ.[7]

Realizing that no weapon that is formed against me will prosper, I will not recompense evil. I will wait on the Lord and He will save me.[8] The Lord God, my heavenly Father, will hold my right hand and say to me, "Do not fear. I will help you."[9] All who will live godly in Christ Jesus shall suffer persecution,[10] but I will not fear when this happens because I dwell in the secret place of the Most High and I abide under the shadow of the Almighty.[11] He is my refuge and my fortress. He is my God, and I will trust Him.[12]

The Lord, my God, will deliver me from the snare of the fowler and from the noisome pestilence.[13] He will cover me with His feathers, and under His wings I will trust. His truth will be my shield and my buckler.[14] I will not fear the terror by night, nor the arrow that flies during the day.[15] I have made the Lord most high my refuge and my habitation.[16]

References: _(1) Romans 8:1; (2) Luke 6:22-23; (3) Matthew 5:44-45; (4) 1 Peter 3:14-16; (5) Psalms 94:22; (6) 1 Peter 2:19-23; (7) Romans 8:29; (8) Proverbs 20:22; (9) Isaiah 41:13; (10) 2 Timothy 3:12; (11) Psalms 91:1; (12) Psalms 91:2; (13) Psalms 91:3; (14) Psalms 91:4; (15) Psalms 91:5; (16) Psalms 91:9._

Bible Prayer: Lord,[1] I thank you for being my refuge.[2] You have promised that because this is so no evil shall befall me.[3] Thank you for being my Father.[4] You are giving your angels charge over me to keep me in all my ways.[5] They will bear me up in their hands to keep me from stumbling.[6]

Thank you, Father, for setting your love upon me, and for delivering me from all evil.

I know you will set me on high because I know your name.[7] When I call upon you, I know you will answer me. You will be with me in trouble. You will deliver me from evil. You will honor me.[8] Thank you, Lord, for the promise of longevity you extend to me.[9] Whenever an evil weapon is raised against me, either from the enemy or from other people, I know it will not prosper, because you have promised to save me.[10] In Jesus' name I pray,[11] Amen.

References: (1) Psalms 92:5; (2) Psalms 91:9; (3) Psalms 91:10; (4) Mark 11:25; (5) Psalms 91:11; (6) Psalms 91:12; (7) Psalms 91:14; (8) Psalms 91:15; (9) Psalms 91:16; (10) 1 John 5:13; (11) John 16:23.

Related Scriptures: 1 Peter 4:14; 1 Peter 4:16; Romans 5:1-2; Matthew 7:1-6; Proverbs 20:22.

57

THE WEAPONS OF MY WARFARE ARE MIGHTY

Bible Promise: "For though we walk in the flesh, we do not war according to the flesh. For the weapons of our warfare are not carnal but mighty in God for pulling down strongholds, casting down arguments and every high thing that exalts itself against the knowledge of God, bringing every thought into captivity to the obedience of Christ" (2 Cor. 10:3-5, NKJV).

Bible Meditation: I am strong in the Lord, and in the power of His might.[1] As I submit myself to God and resist the devil, he flees from me.[2] As I draw near to God, He draws near to me.[3] When I speak the Word[4] and the name of Jesus,[5] the demons have to flee. Jesus has given me spiritual authority that enables me to tread on serpents and scorpions, and over all the power of the enemy. As I use the authority He has delegated to me, I know that nothing shall by any means hurt me.[6]

The Lord preserves me from all evil.[7] Without Him I can do nothing,[8] but through Him I can do all things.[9] I am God's child; therefore, I am an overcomer, because the One who lives in me is greater than the enemy.[10] I will give no place in my life to the devil.[11] I am more than a conqueror through Christ who loves me.[12] God has not given me the spirit of fear, but of power, and of love, and of a sound mind.[13]

Nothing shall be able to separate me from the love of Christ,[14] as I wield the sword of the Spirit,[15] and take the shield of faith with which I will quench all the fiery darts of the wicked one.[16] I will speak the name of Jesus with authority, realizing that everything I request in His name will be given to me.[17] Jesus was manifested in human form so that He could totally destroy the works of the devil, and He lives within me; therefore, I have authority over the devil as well.[18] Through Christ, I will pull down all strongholds, casting down all arguments and every high thing that exalts itself against the knowledge of God, bringing every thought into captivity to the obedience of Christ, my Lord.[19] Hallelujah!

References: *(1) Ephesians 6:10; (2) James 4:7; (3) James 4:8; (4) Luke 4:4; (5) Revelation 12:11; (6) Luke 10:19; (7) Psalms 121:7; (8) John 15:5; (9) Philippians 4:13; (10) 1 John 4:4; (11) Ephesians 4:27; (12) Romans 8:37; (13) 2 Timothy 1:7; (14) Romans 8:39; (15) Ephesians 6:17; (16) Ephesians 6:16; (17) John 16:23; (18) 1 John 3:8, 10; (19) 2 Corinthians 10:3-5.*

Bible Prayer: Heavenly Father,[1] as I walk in the power of your Spirit I will not fulfill the lusts of the flesh.[2] I will be spirtually minded rather than carnally minded so that I will experience your life and peace.[3] I will renew my mind by washing in the water of your Word.[4] I thank you, Father, that the weapons of my spiritual warfare are not carnal. My spiritual weapons are mighty through you. They enable me to tear down every evil stronghold, to cast down arguments and everything that exalts itself against you, and to win the warfare against the enemy.[5]

I choose to bring all my thoughts under captivity to Jesus Christ[6] by thinking on those things that are pure, lovely, and of good report.[7] By meditating on your Word, Father, I am strengthened,[8] and as I pray in the Name of Jesus I gain the power I need to defeat the enemy.[9] Thank you for the power of your Word,[10] the blood of Jesus,[11] the Holy Spirit,[12] and the Name of Jesus Christ.[13] Amen.

References: (1) John 17:1; (2) Galatians 5:16; (3) Romans 8:6; (4) Ephesians 5:26; (5) 2 Corinthians 10:3-5; (6) 2 Corinthians 10:5; (7) Philippians 4:8; (8) Psalms 1; (9) John 14:13-14; (10) Psalms 119:11; (11) Revelation 12:11; (12) Acts 1:8; (13) Philippians 2:9-11.

Related References: 1 John 2:15-17; Romans 12:2; Romans 13:14.

W A Y

58

GOD'S WAY IS PERFECT

Bible Promise: "As for God, his way is perfect: the word of the LORD is tried: he is a buckler to all those that trust in him" (Ps. 18:30).

Bible Meditation: The Word of God is bridging the gap between my ways and God's ways, between His thoughts and my thoughts.[1] For as the heavens are higher than the earth, so are God's ways higher than my ways, and His thoughts than my thoughts.[2]

Jesus has chosen me to be a fruit-bearing believer in the Kingdom of God.[3] He has even invited me to be His friend.[4] I make the personal choice to obey my Lord and Master, and He promises me that I will be more than a servant, I will be His friend, one to whom He reveals all that the Father makes known unto Him.[5] He also promises me that whatever I ask the Father in His name, He will give it to me.[6]

Like Abraham, I want to be a friend of God.[7] Abraham believed God, and his faith was accounted to him as righteousness before God, and God rewarded His faith.[8] My Lord and Savior, Jesus Christ, is a friend that sticks closer than any brother.[9] How I praise Him for His friendship in my life.

As for God, His way is perfect. His Word is dependable.[10] It is through His Word that I learn His ways. A loving reverence for God brings knowledge and wisdom into my life.[11] I know that all things work together for good for me because I love Him and He has called me according to His purpose.[12] The Word of the Lord is proven. I will trust in Him, fully realizing that He is my shield.[13]

The Lord will perfect that which concerns me. His mercy endures forever, and He will never forsake the work of His hands.[14] His Word is a light unto my path and a lamp unto my feet.[15] His Spirit guides me into all truth.[16] Jesus Christ is the way, the truth, and the life.[17]

I will study to show myself approved unto Him, a workman who never needs to be ashamed because I have learned His ways through His Word. I will seek to rightly divide His Word of truth at all times,[18] because I know that the Law (Word) of the Lord is perfect and His testimony is sure, making wise the simple.[19]

References: *(1) Isaiah 55:8; (2) Isaiah 55:9; (3) John 15:16; (4) John 15:14; (5) John 15:15; (6) John 15:16; (7) James 2:23; (8) James 2:23; (9) Proverbs 18:24; (10) Psalms 18:30; (11) Proverbs 1:7; (12) Romans 8:28; (13) Psalms 18:30; (14) Psalms 138:8;*

(15) Psalms 119:105; (16) John 14:71; (17) John 14:6; (18) 2 Timothy 2:15; (19) Psalms 19:7.

Bible Prayer: Lord God,[1] I shall never fear because I know you are with me. I will not be dismayed because I know you are my God. You will strengthen me and help me. You will uphold me with the right hand of your righteousness.[2] I will hold fast the profession of my faith, nothing wavering, because I know that you are faithful to fulfill your promises in my life.[3]

Thank you for your promise to reveal your will and your ways to me. I want to know your ways and to follow them throughout my life because your ways are right, and the just shall walk in them.[4] I want to walk in your ways, Father. Show me your ways, O Lord, and teach me your paths.[5] Lead me in your truth and teach me, for you are the God of my salvation, and on you I wait all day long.[6]

I thank you for your lovingkindness in my life.[7] I will walk in meekness and humility before you so you can teach me your ways.[8] I will walk in reverential fear and worship before you, Father, and I know you will reveal your secrets to me.[9] Reveal all the truths of your covenant to me, Lord.[10] Let integrity and uprightness preserve me as I learn to wait on you.[11] In Jesus' name I pray,[12] Amen.

References: *(1) Exodus 34:23; (2) Isaiah 41:18; (3) Hebrews 10:23; (4) Hosea 14:9; (5) Psalms 25:4; (6) Psalms 25:5; (7) Psalms 25:6; (8) Psalms 25:9; (9) Psalms 25:14; (10) Psalms 25:14; (11) Psalms 25:21; (12) John 16:23.*

Related Scriptures: *Psalms 119:3; Psalms 145:17; Isaiah 2:3; Micah 4:2.*

59

I AM COMPLETE IN CHRIST

Bible Promise: "For in him dwelleth all the fullness of the Godhead bodily. And ye are complete in him, which is the head of all principality and power" (Col. 2:9-10).

Bible Meditation: In the same way that I have received Jesus Christ as my Lord and Savior, I will walk in Him.[1] It is my desire to be rooted and built up in Him and established in the faith as I have been taught, with thanksgiving.[2] He is filling me with the knowledge of His will in all wisdom and spiritual understanding so that I may walk worthy of the Lord, fully pleasing unto Him and fruitful in every good work, increasing in the knowledge of God.[3] He is strengthening me with all might, according to His glorious power, unto all patience and longsuffering with joyfulness.[4]

My heart is thankful to the Father for all He has done for me. He made me able to partake of the inheritance of the saints in light.[5] He has delivered me from the power of darkness and translated me into the kingdom of His dear Son, my Lord and Savior, Jesus Christ.[6] Through the blood of Jesus I have redemption and all my sins have been forgiven.[7] Jesus is the perfect image of God, the firstborn of every creature.[8] By Him all things in heaven and in earth were created. They were created by Him and for Him.[9] He is before all things, and in Him all things hold together.[10] He is the Head of the Body, His Church. He is the beginning,[11] the first and the last.[12] He is the Alpha and the Omega.[13]

It pleased the Father to let all fullness dwell within His Son,[14] and, having made peace through the blood of the cross, God has, through Jesus, reconciled all things unto himself.[15] It is through this great redemption that I have been made complete in Him,[16] and in all things in my life I want Jesus Christ to have the preeminence.[17]

References: (1) Colossians 2:6; (2) Colossians 2:7; (3) Colossians 1:9-10; (4) Colossians 1:11; (5) Colossians 1:12; (6) Colossians 1:13; (7) Colossians 1:14; (8) Colossians 1:15; (9) Colossians 1:16; (10) Colossians 1:17; (11) Colossians 1:18; (12) Revelation 1:11; (13) Revelation 1:11; (14) Colossians 1:19; (15) Colossians 1:20; (16) Colossians 2:10; (17) Colossians 1:18.

Bible Prayer: Dear Lord,[1] your Word asks me to be perfect as you are perfect.[2] I realize that I cannot perfect myself, but I know I can do all things through Christ who strengthens me.[3] Through Him, who is complete in every respect,

I can stand perfect and complete in all your will.[4] Thank you, Father.

Through Christ I am justified — just as if I'd never sinned.[5] He is my righteousness.[6] My wholeness is in Him, and because I am complete in Him, I will never waver about your special promises to me through unbelief. I will be strong in faith, giving glory to you at all times.

I am fully persuaded that what you promise to me you will perform, and it is this strong faith that gives me righteousness and completion in Jesus Christ[7] who was delivered for my offenses and was raised again for my justification.[8] I believe your Word, Father, and I know you raised Jesus from the dead.[9] In His name I pray,[10] Amen.

References: *(1) 1 Chronicles 16:26; (2) Matthew 5:48; (3) Philippians 4:13; (4) Colossians 4:12; (5) Titus 3:7; (6) Romans 4:6; (7) Romans 4:20-23; (8) Romans 4:25; (9) Romans 4:25; (10) John 15:16.*

Related Scriptures: *Matthew 19:21; John 17:23; 2 Corinthians 12:9; 2 Corinthians 13:11; 2 Timothy 3:17; 1 Peter 5:10.*

60

GOD GIVES ME THE POWER TO WITNESS

Bible Promise: "But you shall receive power when the Holy Spirit has come upon you; and you shall be witnesses to Me ..." (Acts 1:8, NKJV).

Bible Meditation: The Spirit of God is upon me.[1] He empowers me to be a witness for my Lord and Savior, Jesus Christ, wherever I go — at home, at work, in the neighborhood, in the marketplace, and even in church.[2] Through His power, I am an effective ambassador for Jesus Christ.[3]

Realizing that a person who wins souls is wise,[4] I commit myself to being a vibrant witness for my Lord and Savior.[5] He will lead me[6] to the ones who need Him, and He will give me the right words to say.[7]

This is my commission as His disciple, a mandate from my heavenly Father — to go into the world and teach all nations.[8] With the power of the Holy Spirit filling me, I will not be ashamed of the Gospel of Jesus Christ because I know it is the power of God unto salvation to all who believe.[9]

I will go to the highways and byways of this busy world in an effort to find those who need the Savior.[10] As I do so, He will guide me each step of the way.[11] His perfect love casts out all fear while I witness.[12] My goal is to reach the lost, to rescue the perishing, and to care for the dying.

I am the salt of the earth,[13] and I want my life to make others thirsty for Jesus. I am the light of the world,[14] and I want my life to reflect God's light to others. I will be a witness for Jesus Christ throughout this day, and I receive His enabling power to be His representative wherever I go.[15]

References: *(1) Luke 4:18; (2) Acts 1:8; (3) 2 Corinthians 5:20; (4) Proverbs 11:30; (5) Isaiah 43:12; (6) Psalms 5:8; (7) Mark 13:11; (8) Matthew 28:19-20; (9) Romans 1:16; (10) Luke 14:23; (11) Psalms 48:14; (12) 1 John 4:18; (13) Matthew 5:13; (14) Matthew 5:14; (15) Ephesians 6:20.*

Bible Prayer: Fill me with your Spirit, Father.[1] Through Him, I will be a witness to others.[2] Give me wisdom[3] that will enable me to know when I should speak and when I should remain silent, to know with whom I should share your gospel, and to know what I should say.[4] I know you will give me this wisdom liberally,[5] because you are the Giver of every good and perfect gift.[6]

Help me to develop a sensitivity to others that will permit me to hear the cries of their hearts,[7] even as you do, Father.[8] Give me empathy for those I witness to, and help me to assure each one that you understand and love them.[9] Let your powerful love flow through me and reach out to others.[10] In Jesus' name I pray,[11] Amen.

References: (1) Ephesians 5:18; (2) Acts 1:8; (3) James 1:5; (4) Matthew 10:19; (5) James 1:5; (6) James 1:17; (7) Galatians 6:1-2; (8) Psalms 18:6; (9) Hebrews 4:15-16; (10) 1 John 4:11; (11) John 15:16.

Related Scriptures: Psalms 107:2; John 1:12; John 1:34; John 5:39; Acts 4:33; Acts 10:43; Romans 1:16; Ephesians 6:20; 2 Corinthians 5:20.

61

GOD'S WORD IS POWERFUL

Bible Promise: "For the word of God is quick, and powerful, and sharper than any twoedged sword, piercing even to the dividing asunder of soul and spirit, and of the joints and marrow, and is a discerner of the thoughts and intents of the heart" (Heb. 4:12).

Bible Meditation: The Word of God is a lamp unto my feet and a light unto my path.[1] It is living and powerful,[2] and it imparts faith to my heart.[3] I will study it diligently so I can be a worker who does not need to be ashamed, but rightly divides God's Word.[4] All Scripture is given by God's inspiration and it provides me with doctrine, reproof, correction, and instruction in righteousness so that I will be able to do good works for my Lord.[5]

I realize that I do not live by bread alone, but by every word that proceeds from the mouth of God.[6] His Word declares that I have power over the enemy.[7] His Word is truth, and it sanctifies me.[8] The Word of God renews my mind.[9] It is the sword of the Spirit.[10] God's Word keeps me from sin.[11] I will hide God's Word in my heart so that I will not sin against Him.[12]

The Word of God has the power to heal me and to deliver me from all negative influences in my life. This truth inspires me to praise the Lord for His goodness, and for His wonderful works in my life.[13] God's testimonies are wonderful, and my soul will treasure them and keep them.[14] When His Word enters my spirit, it fills me with light and it gives me understanding.[15] His Word brings cleansing to my soul.[16]

When I was born again it was by the incorruptible seed of the Word of God which lives and abides forever.[17] His Word endures forever.[18] In the beginning was the Word, and the Word was with God, and the Word was God. Jesus is the living Word of God. All things were made by Him, and without Him was not anything made that was made. In Him was life, and the life was the light of men.[19] There is great power in the Word of God.[20]

References: (1) *Psalms 119:105;* (2) *Hebrews 4:12;* (3) *Romans 10:17;* (4) *2 Timothy 2:15;* (5) *2 Timothy 3:16-17;* (6) *Matthew 4:4;* (7) *Luke 4;* (8) *John 17:17;* (9) *Ephesians 5:26;* (10) *Ephesians 6:17;* (11) *Psalms 119:11;* (12) *Psalms 119:11;* (13) *Psalms 107:20-21;* (14) *Psalms 119:129;* (15) *Psalms 119:130;* (16) *John 15:3;* (17) *1 Peter 1:23;* (18) *1 Peter 1:25;* (19) *John 1:1-4;* (20) *2 Peter 3:5.*

Bible Prayer: Teach me, O Lord, the ways of your Word. I will keep your statutes to the end.[1] Give me understanding and I will keep your law. I want to observe your Word with all my heart.[2] Lead me in the paths of your commandments, for in your Word I find my delight.[3] Incline my heart   to your Word.[4] Establish your Word within me.[5] I trust in your Word.[6] By seeking the truth of your Word I know I will be able to walk in freedom.[7]

Your Word has given me life.[8] I will keep your Word.[9] Thank you for your Word, Father, I know that it is established forever in the heavens.[10] How I love your Word! I will meditate upon it all day long.[11] How sweet are your words to my taste; your Word is sweeter than honey.[12] Your Word is pure like silver that has been tried in an earthen furnace and has been purified seven times. I praise you, Father, that the power of your Word will be preserved from this generation and forevermore.[13]

References: (1) *Psalms 119:33; (2) Psalms 119:34; (3) Psalms 119:35; (4) Psalms 119:36; (5) Psalms 119:38; (6) Psalms 119:42; (7) Psalms 119:45; (8) Psalms 119:50; (9) Psalms 119:57; (10) Psalms 119:89; (11) Psalms 119:97; (12) Psalms 119:103; (13) Psalms 12:6-7.*

Related Scriptures: *Psalms 130:5; John 5:24; 1 Peter 2:2-3; 1 Peter 1:23-25; Luke 21:33; John 6:63; Hebrews 11:3; Isaiah 40:8.*

62

MY WORDS ARE POWERFUL

Bible Promise: "The tongue has the power of life and death, and those who love it will eat its fruit" (Prov. 18:21, NIV).

Bible Meditation: The words of my mouth are like deep waters and the wellspring of wisdom is like a flowing brook.[1] Realizing that a fool's mouth is his destruction and his lips build a trap for his soul,[2] I will let my words be few,[3] because I know that in the multitude of words sin can always be found.[4] With God's help, I will bridle my tongue.[5]

I will always endeavor to speak out of the abundance of my heart,[6] where I have hidden God's Word,[7] so that I will always declare the way of the Lord,[8] and speak His truth with my lips.[9] It is by my words that I will be justified.[10]

My heart is a wellspring of wisdom because Jesus lives there, and He gives sweetness to my lips that helps me to increase in learning.[11] My heart teaches my mouth what to say.[12] Pleasant words are as an honeycomb; they are sweet to my soul and they give me health.[13] I will speak God's Word from my heart to my mind and through my lips; when I do so and obey the commandments of the Lord, the angels hearken to my voice speaking God's Word.[14]

God's Word is near me; it is in my mouth and in my heart. It is the Word of faith that enabled me to confess with my mouth that Jesus Christ is my Lord. I believe in my heart that God has raised Him from the dead, and I am saved.[15] With my heart I believe unto righteousness and with my mouth I make confession unto salvation.[16]

Therefore, as I believe I will speak.[17] Hearing God's Word builds faith in my heart,[18] and I will speak His Word.[19] When I speak the Word of God to the mountain in prayer, as the Holy Spirit prompts me, I will have whatever I say.[20] When I speak the Word of God by faith I will have spiritual authority in every situation.[21]

My words are powerful.[22] The tongue of the wise is health.[23] I shall eat good as a result of the fruit of my mouth.[24] By guarding my mouth I will be able to preserve my life.[25] I will use my tongue to bless the Lord at all times.[26] I will let His praise be continually in my mouth.[27] I will speak His truth in love.[28] I will speak what I believe from the Word of God,[29] I will speak whatever God commands, for I trust in Him with all my heart and lean not to my own understanding. In all my ways I acknowledge Him and I know He will direct my paths.[30]

References: (1) Proverbs 18:4; (2) Proverbs 18:7; (3) Ecclesiastes 5:2; (4) Proverbs 10:19; (5) James 3:2; (6) Matthew 12:34; (7) Psalms 119:11; (8) Psalms 119:26; (9) Psalms 119:43; (10) Matthew 12:37; (11) Proverbs 16:23; (12) Proverbs 16:23; (13) Proverbs 16:24; (14) Psalms 103:20; (15) Romans 10:8-9; (16) Romans 10:10; (17) 2 Corinthians 4:13; (18) Romans 10:17; (19) Romans 10:10; (20) Mark 11:23; (21) Luke 17:6; (22) Proverbs 18:21; (23) Proverbs 12:18; (24) Proverbs 13:2; (25) Proverbs 13:3; (26) James 3:9; (27) Psalms 34:1; (28) Ephesians 4:15; (29) 2 Corinthians 4:13; (30) Proverbs 3:5-6.

Bible Prayer: Dear Lord,[1] I will praise you.[2] My heart is established in your Word.[3] My heart is fixed; I trust in you.[4] I will walk in your ways.[5] I will keep your Word and seek you with all my heart.[6] With my lips I will declare your judgments,[7] and I will not forget your Word.[8] Teach me your statutes so I can declare your ways.[9] Help me to understand your precepts so I can talk of all your wondrous works.[10] Strengthen me according to your Word.[11] I will speak of your testimonies.[12] I will rise to thank you for the power of your Word.[13]

I will speak your Word because it is better to me than gold and silver.[14] Your Word is forever settled in heaven.[15] Oh, how I love your Word.[16] It is a lamp unto my feet and a light unto my path.[17] It is the rejoicing of my heart.[18] My lips will utter praise to you,[19] and my tongue shall speak your Word.[20] In Jesus' name I pray,[21] Amen.

References: (1) Psalms 118:28; (2) Psalms 113:1; (3) Psalms 112:8; (4) Psalms 112:7; (5) Psalms 119:1; (6) Psalms 119:2; (7) Psalms 119:13; (8) Psalms 119:16; (9) Psalms 119:26; (10) Psalms 119:27; (11) Psalms 119:28; (12) Psalms 119:46; (13) Psalms 119:62; (14) Psalms 119:72; (15) Psalms 119:89; (16) Psalms 119:97; (17) Psalms 119:107; (18) Psalms 119:111; (19) Psalms 119:171; (20) Psalms 119:172; (21) John 15:16.

Related Scriptures: Psalms 149:6; Proverbs 21:23; Isaiah 1:20; Jeremiah 1:9; Ephesians 4:29; Colossians 3:8.